Holy Land, 1
Sacred Geograp~~hy and the~~
Interpretation of the Bible

Didsbury Lectures, 2001

Holy Land, Holy City
Sacred Geography and the Interpretation of the Bible

Robert P. Gordon

PATERNOSTER

Copyright © 2004 Robert P. Gordon
First published in 2004 by Paternoster Press

09 08 07 06 05 04   7 6 5 4 3 2 1

Paternoster Press is an imprint of Authentic Media,
P.O. Box 300, Carlisle, Cumbria, CA3 0QS, UK
and
P.O. Box 1047, Waynesboro, GA 30830-2047, USA
Website: www.paternoster-publishing.com

British Library Cataloguing in Publication Data
A catalogue record for this book is available from the British Library

ISBN 1-84227-277-2

Cover Design by FourNineZero
Typeset by WestKey Ltd, Falmouth, Cornwall
Print Management by Adare Carwin
Printed by J. H. Haynes & Co. Ltd, Sparkford

For Alasdair

Contents

Preface

An impressive list of worthies has contributed to the Didsbury Lectures since their inception in 1979 when F.F. Bruce lectured on 'Men and Movements in the Primitive Church'. Nevertheless, I accepted the invitation to give the series for 2001, and the kindness shown to me during the 'Didsbury Week' (29 October to 1 November) by Herbert McGonigle, Principal of Nazarene Theological College, his colleagues and their spouses remains a lively and pleasant memory. The material delivered on the four evenings of the lectures has now been rearranged and divided among seven, mainly short, chapters. Two other items help make up the total of nine chapters. Chapter 7, entitled 'Marching to Zion', presents the text of the Fifth Annual Semitic Studies Lecture delivered at The Queen's University, Belfast, on 6 March 2003. Due acknowledgement is made in the footnotes there. Chapter 9 represents the gist of a morning chapel talk given during the course of the 'Didsbury Week' – an occasion also remembered for the period of rousing 'one-way praise' that preceded the talk.

I first explored the theme of geography and biblical interpretation in a paper read at the summer meeting of the Society for Old Testament Study in Glasgow in 1999, but it was clear then that the disparate types of material lightly touched upon needed fuller treatment in a different format. In certain respects the effort has been an indulgence, as I have pursued topics of strong personal interest that at one or two points have exceeded my normal academic range, as for example in chapter 5 on Golgotha. Chapter 8, on the interpretation of (especially) land issues, took me into a minefield that I regarded as unavoidable if important hermeneutical aspects of 'Bible geography' were not to be neglected. On such delicate matters it would be comforting for me to regard what I have written as carrying implications rather than offering conclusions, but the reader had better decide. In their different ways the various chapters illustrate the importance of non-literal geography for both Testaments, but I suspect that some readers may fare better if they pass quickly over the first four chapters, dealing with issues perhaps of more interest to Old Testament specialists, and concentrate on chapters 5 to 9. All readers should be grateful to Robin Parry and Tony Graham of Paternoster Press for a number of interventions on their behalf before the manuscript was put to bed. My thanks also go to Leslie McFall for his assistance in compiling the bibliography and indexes.

This study is dedicated with affection to Alasdair (aka 'Ali'), the family's Benjamin, who recently marked his eighteenth birthday with a weeklong celebration worthy of the best biblical festivals.

Comberton, Cambridge
10 October 2003

Abbreviations

AB	The Anchor Bible
ANET	J.B. Pritchard (ed.), *Ancient Near Eastern Texts Relating to the Old Testament* (3rd edn, 1969)
Ant.	Josephus' *Jewish Antiquities*
ASOR	American Schools of Oriental Research
ATD	Das Alte Testament Deutsch
b.	Babylonian Talmud
BA	*Biblical Archaeologist*
BDB	F. Brown, S.R. Driver and C.A. Briggs, *A Hebrew and English Lexicon of the Old Testament* (1906)
BH	Biblical Hebrew
BHS	*Biblia Hebraica Stuttgartensia*
BKAT	Biblischer Kommentar: Altes Testament
CAD	*The Assyrian Dictionary of the Oriental Institute of the University of Chicago*
CBOTS	Coniectanea Biblica, Old Testament Series
CBQ	*Catholic Biblical Quarterly*
CCSL	Corpus Christianorum, Series Latina
DJD	*Discoveries in the Judaean Desert*
EH	Eusebius' *Ecclesiastical History*
HALAT	*The Hebrew and Aramaic Lexicon of the Old Testament* (Eng. tr. M.E.J. Richardson)
HUCA	*Hebrew Union College Annual*
ICC	The International Critical Commentary
IEJ	*Israel Exploration Journal*
JBL	*Journal of Biblical Literature*
JNSL	*Journal of Northwest Semitic Languages*
JQR	*Jewish Quarterly Review*
JSJ	*Journal for the Study of Judaism*
JSOT	*Journal for the Study of the Old Testament*
JSP	*Journal for the Study of the Pseudepigrapha*
JTS	*Journal of Theological Studies*
KAT	Kommentar zum Alten Testament

LXX	The 'Septuagint' Greek Version of the Old Testament
m.	Mishnah
MQ	Mo^ced Qatan
MT	Masoretic Text
NS	New Series
PEFQS	*Palestine Exploration Fund Quarterly Statement*
Pes.	Pesachim
PG	J.-P. Migne, *Patrologia Graeca*
PL	J.-P. Migne, *Patrologia Latina*
RB	*Revue Biblique*
ScrHieros	*Scripta Hierosolymitana*
SJSOT	Supplements to *Journal for the Study of the Old Testament*
SNTSMS	Society for New Testament Studies Monograph Series
SVT	Supplements to *Vetus Testamentum*
VT	*Vetus Testamentum*
WBC	Word Biblical Commentary
WUNT	Wissenschaftliche Untersuchungen zum Neuen Testament
ZAW	*Zeitschrift für die alttestamentliche Wissenschaft*

Introduction

Geography – mainly of the 'sacred' variety – and 'Sacred Space' are the topics that link the several chapters of this study. 'Sacred Geography' is, of course, a term that is used variously. Traditionally, in the Judeo-Christian world, it relates to sites and regions that feature in the Bible and are deemed 'sacred' on that account.[1] But under this heading we may also find, with the help of a bibliographical trawl, such diverse topics as prehistoric sacred geography,[2] zodiacal coordinates and astrological symbolism among the ancient Greeks,[3] the thought-world of American mound-builders,[4] places venerated in American spirituality for their capacity to mediate 'the holy',[5] and Buddhist mandalas representing sanctified realms and used as an aid to meditation.[6]

Basically, what I call 'Sacred Geography' comes into play when the literal, geographical facts of a case are disregarded by a biblical

---

[1] E.g. *Sacred Geography, contained in six maps* (London: printed for J. Senex and W. Taylor, 1716). The six maps cover the location of Paradise and countries inhabited by the patriarchs, peoples of the world after Noah and Israel's journeys in the wilderness, the plan of Jerusalem and the temple of Solomon, the holy land divided among the twelve tribes, the land of 'Canaan' as travelled by Christ and his apostles, and the travels of Paul and the other apostles.

[2] Josef Heinsch, *Principles of Prehistoric Sacred Geography* (tr. M. Behrend; Bar Hill: Fenris-Wolf, 1977).

[3] Jean Richer, *Sacred Geography of the Ancient Greeks: Astrological Symbolism in Art, Architecture, and Landscape* (tr. Christine Rhone; Albany, NY: State University of New York Press, 1994).

[4] Maureen Korp, *The Sacred Geography of the American Mound Builders* (Native American Studies, 2; Lewiston/Lampeter: Edwin Mellen Press, 1990).

[5] Belden C. Lane, *Landscapes of the Sacred: Geography and Narrative in American Spirituality* (Isaac Hecker Studies in Religion and American Culture; New York: Paulist Press, 1988).

[6] Elizabeth ten Grotenhuis, *Japanese Mandalas: Representations of Sacred Geography* (Honolulu: University of Hawaii, 1999).

text in order to express some further, or higher, truth. Even in ordinary map-making we are familiar with the idea of strictly non-literal representation of the geography of our own planet. The long favoured Mercator projection devised by the Flemish geographer Gerhard Kremer in the sixteenth century functions only by partly misrepresenting reality, showing areas near the equator more accurately than those nearer the poles. The element of misrepresentation is not deliberate, but simply reflects the difficulty of reducing a globe to a flat page. On the other hand, one of the world's oldest maps possibly illustrates the *ideological* potential in map-making: in the famous Babylonian *mappa mundi* Babylon is represented by a generous rectangle, whereas Assyria receives a small oval.[7] At the least, the Babylonian provenance of the map is confirmed by the prominence that it gives to Babylon. In the present study the actual term 'Sacred Geography' occurs infrequently outside this introduction; even so, discussion throughout will focus on geography in the service of religion and theology.

'Sacred Geography' overlaps with the concept of 'Sacred Space', but takes in a lot more. It moves beyond geographical literality in the way that 'Sacred Time' (or what might be called 'Sacred Chronology') transcends ordinary chronological time. We might describe it as merely a form of 'hyperbole', but if we do not distinguish it from hyperbole we risk missing its fuller implications in any given text. The point can be illustrated from Isaiah 41:2, 9, 25 where, in contrast to Cyrus, the Persian conqueror, who is described as coming from the east (v. 2) or the north (v. 25), the people of Israel, in the persons of the patriarchs, are said to have been summoned by God 'from the ends of the earth', 'from its farthest corners' (v. 9). In strictly geographical terms, Cyrus came from further east than Abraham or any of the patriarchs, but the point of the statement is that the manner and the implications of God's choice of Israel transcend all such literality. What God first set about doing when he called Abraham, he continues to do, and what he is doing for Israel eclipses even the spectacular rise of Cyrus, though this too is seen as part of the activity of God in the world (Isa. 41:4).

The nine chapters in this study fall into two groupings. Chapters 1–4 are straightforwardly about Old Testament texts and themes

---

[7] See W. Horowitz, 'The Babylonian Map of the World', *Iraq* 50 (1988), 147–65(148–49); idem, *Mesopotamian Cosmic Geography* (Mesopotamian Civilizations, 8; Winona Lake: Eisenbrauns, 1998), 21, 26. The map is not older than the ninth century ('The Babylonian Map', 153; *Mesopotamian Cosmic Geography*, 25).

relating to the 'holy land' and 'holy city'. History, as well as geography, plays a part here. First, it is observed in chapter 1 that, whatever the proper genre of Genesis 1–11, these chapters have a serious historiographical aspect to them, and that this most likely explains why all reference to Jerusalem/Zion is excluded from their account of beginnings. Secondly, the issue of history or non-history inevitably arises in chapter 4 in the discussion of Psalm 48. It is concluded there that the presence of mythical – but more especially of hyperbolical – elements in the laudation of Zion and its God does not exclude the psalm's having been composed in celebration of a national deliverance from danger.

In chapter 2, on the other hand, it is suggested that the anachronistic concept of the 'holy land' – perhaps more a matter of 'Sacred Space' than of 'Sacred Geography' – has been introduced into the story of Cain and Abel in order to help define Cain's punishment in relation to the foregoing expulsion of Adam and Eve from Eden. In chapter 3 the absentee 'holy city' of the opening chapter comes into plain view. It becomes clear that the biblical tradition resists the scaling down of Israel's God to the status of a typical near eastern city god, hence the rarity of the expression 'the God of Jerusalem' in the Old Testament. Conversely, Jerusalem is the 'City of God', though its unique standing does not win it 'link-city' status in the way of major Mesopotamian temple-cities; nor does a Jerusalem 'omphalos mythology' develop until post-biblical times.

The second grouping of chapters begins with 'The Geography of Golgotha' (ch. 5), which topic seems to strike out in a different direction from what has preceded. However, the tendency of early Christian writers to apply to Golgotha symbolism and significances originally belonging to Jerusalem/Zion means that themes from earlier chapters are resurrected at this point. 'Future Dimensions' (ch. 6) notes how another kind of transposition has already taken place within the Old Testament, where the hyperbolizing of the historical Jerusalem/Zion assumes new proportions in the prophetic envisioning of the 'holy city' and 'holy land' in relation to the end-time. However, end-time is preceded by 'meantime', and for both the Jewish and Christian traditions pilgrimage has played an important part in preserving the past associations of sacred sites, deriving present benefit from attendance at them, and anticipating the realization of the ultimate hope to which they bear witness (ch. 7). In chapter 8 discussion evolves from Zion to Zionism, the biblical land promises and their relevance, if any, for current issues and possible future developments in Israel/Palestine. The chapter concludes with a postscript on the human costs of misinterpreting texts that are heavy in symbolism and vulnerable to ignorance and *parti pris*. The final chapter, on Christ's meeting with the Samaritan woman at the well of Sychar, highlights the 'a-territorial' nature of Christian worship of God, when, with the sidelining of 'place' and the politics of 'place', profounder insights and broader vistas become possible.

Chapter One

Absent City/Missing Mountains in Genesis 1–11

Absent City

'Sacred Geography' is, I suggest, a useful category to bring to the study of Genesis 1–11, the so-called 'Primeval History',[1] even if, a little perversely, the subject has to be discussed 'in the negative', since it is the *absence* of an eligible candidate for inclusion that attracts attention here. The significant absentee is Jerusalem. As we shall see, there are good reasons why we might have expected early Genesis to include at least allusions to Jerusalem/Zion, despite the anachronism involved, in recognition of the city's subsequent importance in Israelite history. This absence has not, to my knowledge, been much discussed in connection with Genesis 1–11, though the situation in the rest of the Pentateuch, from the patriarchal stories on, has been noted and debated by a number of writers.

First, however, we should note that the earliest epigraphic reference to Jerusalem comes in the Egyptian Execration Texts, which are dated to the early second millennium BC and include mentions of Jerusalem and two of its rulers.[2] From the Late Bronze Age, we have letters from Abdu-Hepa king of 'Urusalim' surviving in the fourteenth-century Amarna archives.[3] There was, therefore, an early city of Jerusalem already in the second millennium. On the other hand, Jerusalem is absent even from the biblical 'Table of Nations' in Genesis 10. Since this list reflects ethnic and political realities of periods later than its setting would suggest, it would be reasonable for Jerusalem to feature in it. The Table mentions not only Babylon and Nineveh, but also a number of other ancient cities

---

[1] It is convenient to treat the whole of Genesis 1–11 as a 'Primeval (or Proto-) History', even though some others put the full stop after the account of the flood and its aftermath (i.e., at 9:17 or 9:29).
[2] See *ANET*, 329.
[3] See *ANET*, 487–89.

of varying degrees of importance (vv. 10–12, 19). And there are other grounds for surprise at this absence of Jerusalem not only from the 'Table of Nations' but also from Genesis 1–11 as a whole.

In the first place, Jerusalem became as ideologically favoured as any city in the ancient world, and certainly as much as Babylon. For Babylon that meant that even early human history could be constructed in such a way as to express the city's claim to supremacy in the world-order of the ancient near east. Historical scruples did not prevent the officially sanctioned creation account *Enuma Elish* from securing a place for Babylon at the creation and before the flood. There is no evidence that Babylon played a part in the history of third millennium Sumer, nor is it to Babylon that kingship 'descends' in the Sumerian King List,[4] yet in tablet 6 of *Enuma Elish* the creation of humans is followed by the proposal of the Anunnaki to build a sanctuary for Marduk, who gratefully accepts the suggestion with the command, 'Build Babylon' (line 57).[5] Even in Genesis 1–11, it will be recalled, there is a place for Babylon – not only in the 'Table of Nations' (cf. 10:10), but also in 11:1–9 which, with its satire on the building of Babel, testifies to the 'primeval pretensions' of Babylonian royal and priestly propaganda in the historical period.

A second reason why we might have expected allusion to Jerusalem/Zion in early Genesis is the apparent connection made in the Old Testament psalmic tradition between Jerusalem and the Genesis paradise, in the mention of the river 'whose streams make glad the city of God' (Ps. 46:5[4]). In the context there is not much doubt about the city, yet Jerusalem is notoriously ill-served where riverine irrigation is concerned. The only 'river' in its vicinity is a wadi, the Kidron. Certainly, when Ezekiel 47 and Zechariah 14 talk of copious supplies of water issuing from the new Jerusalem, or its temple, they deal more convincingly in eschatological symbolism than in Judean hydrography.[6] This is also the case in Isaiah 33:21,

---

[4] Cf. T. Jacobsen, *The Sumerian King List* (Assyriological Studies, 11; Chicago: University of Chicago Press, 1939), 70–71; H. Frankfort, *Kingship and the Gods: A Study of Ancient Near Eastern Religion as the Integration of Society and Nature* (Chicago: University of Chicago Press, 1948), 242. See also M. Civil, 'The Sumerian Flood Story', in W.G. Lambert and A.R. Millard (eds.), *Atra-ḫasīs: The Babylonian Story of the Flood* (Oxford: Clarendon Press, 1969), 138–45(140–41).

[5] As noted by S. Sykes, *Time and Space in Haggai-Zechariah 1–8: A Bakhtinian Analysis of a Prophetic Chronicle* (Studies in Biblical Literature, 24; New York: Lang, 2002), 60–61.

[6] It is sometimes surmised that Ezekiel's temple river has the Kidron in mind, since this latter, like Ezekiel's river, runs down to the Dead Sea, taking the name Wadi en-Nar in its later stages (cf. W.R. Farmer, 'The Geography of Ezekiel's River of Life', *BA* 19 [1956], 17–22[19]).

where the Jerusalem of the future is envisaged as 'a place of broad rivers and streams'. So it is commonly understood that in Psalm 46:5(4) the river of paradise (cf. Gen. 2:10–14) has been 'redirected' to the Jerusalem area for the delectation of the holy city, now described in idealized contrast with the environmental and political commotions mentioned in the surrounding verses. The fact that one of the four distributaries of the river of paradise shares the name Gihon with the well-known spring to the east of Jerusalem may support the connection between Jerusalem and Eden suggested for Psalm 46 (see Gen. 2:13; 2 Chr. 32:30). The Jerusalemite Gihon provided the city with essential water, and on a famous occasion received the attentions of King Hezekiah when he constructed his tunnel from Gihon to Siloam.[7] But even if the psalmist had the Gihon spring itself in mind, as has been suggested by, for example, Lang, it no less than the Kidron would require to be hyperbolized in order to answer to the terms of Psalm 46:5(4).[8]

The third reason for commenting on the absence of Jerusalem/Zion from early Genesis is that later Jewish tradition associates Jerusalem with creation. Creation started from Zion, which represented the perfection of earthly beauty, according to the Babylonian Talmud (b. Yoma 54b). Again, it was 'from the place of the temple' that light was created, according to the Midrash on Genesis (Gen. r. 3:4).[9] This 'mythologizing' of Jerusalem necessarily overlooks the city's pre-Israelite phase, as it extends the significance of both city and temple right back to the creation of the world.

---

[7] See J.D. Levenson, *Sinai and Zion: An Entry into the Jewish Bible* (New Voices in Biblical Studies; Minneapolis: Winston Press, 1985), 130–32.

[8] B. Lang, *The Hebrew God: Portrait of an Ancient Deity* (New Haven and London: Yale University Press, 2002), 166 ('this spring's quasi-mythological status'). The contrary view is taken by R.J. Clifford, *The Cosmic Mountain in Canaan and the Old Testament* (Harvard Semitic Monographs, 4; Cambridge, MA: Harvard University Press, 1972), 101, who thinks that the Pishon and Gihon rivers are introduced artificially into Genesis 2:10–14 in order to make up, with the Tigris and Euphrates, a riverine quartet representing a geographical totality as in the expression 'the four quarters (of the earth)': 'the Gihon in Gen. 2 need not be the spring of Jerusalem' (ibid., fn. 5). For obvious obstacles to a literal identification of the Gihon of Genesis 2 with the Jerusalem spring see S. Tuell, 'The Rivers of Paradise: Ezekiel 47:1–12 and Genesis 2:10–14', in William P. Brown and S. Dean McBride (eds.), *God Who Creates: Essays in Honor of W. Sibley Towner* (Grand Rapids and Cambridge: Eerdmans, 2000), 171–89(178). Considerations of a 'Sacred Geography' type, however, incline Tuell to think that the Gihon of paradise may relate after a fashion to the spring located just outside Jerusalem: 'Genesis 2, like Ezekiel 47, belongs to the realm of the supramundane' (178–89).

[9] Cf. Levenson, *Sinai and Zion*, 133.

Fourthly, the absence of Jerusalem from Genesis 1–11 is the more apparent when we consider the Endzeit/Urzeit relation of the last two chapters of the New Testament Apocalypse to Genesis 1–3. The echoes of early Genesis in these chapters are clear, yet, since Revelation 21–22 is mainly an account of the New Jerusalem, in this respect at least Endzeit cannot match Urzeit, there being no Jerusalem in Genesis 1–3.

Explaining Absent Zion

As we shall have cause to note,[10] later Hebrew thought categories are anachronistically present in Genesis 1–11; and still there is little justification for seeing Zion or Zion mythology in these chapters. Indeed, those writers who interpret the paradise story or the Babel narrative as critique of royalist pretensions in Judah, or as a caricature of Jerusalem, 'with its city and tower built by men's hands',[11] are claiming to find *anti*-Zion elements in the narrative.

Any of several factors may help account for the absence of Jerusalem/Zion from Genesis 1–3(11). The first is that of a history-like approach that did not wish to fly in the face of the tradition – deeply entrenched in the historical books of the Old Testament – that Jerusalem remained a Jebusite enclave until the time of David.[12] Its incorporation into the Israelite kingdom came relatively late, as the account of its capture in 2 Samuel 5 suggests. Secondly, the holy mountain concept, for all that it was adopted by the theologians of Jerusalem and Judah, is absent from Genesis 1–3, possibly as part of an anti-mythological programme in these and later chapters. There are conspicuous anti-mythological and anti-heroic elements in the Primeval History (cf. 6:1–4; 11:1–9). Thirdly, cities do not fare well

---

[10] See ch. 2.

[11] T.L. Thompson, *The Bible in History: How Writers Create a Past* (London: Jonathan Cape, 1999), 42 (cf. 262).

[12] The biblical tradition about the conquest of Jebus-Jerusalem may reflect a more general outlook on the part of Old Testament writers, according to which places were regarded as sacred on the basis of divine choice rather than of immemorial sanctity: 'for the Old Testament, as far as I can see, the holiness of a place tends to be a quality acquired through becoming in history a place of divine manifestation rather than an inherent quality it has had from primaeval times. Zion is not a holy place since the *Urzeit*, but has become a holy place – for Israel – with experienced time' (D.J.A. Clines, 'Sacred Space, Holy Places and Suchlike', in *On the Way to the Postmodern: Old Testament Essays, 1967–1998. Volume II* [SJSOT 293; Sheffield: Sheffield Academic Press, 1998], 542–54[548–49]).

in early Genesis:[13] Cain rebels against his sentence to nomady by building a city and naming it after his son (4:17);[14] city building is part of the agenda at Babel, where the builders are punished for their efforts; the whole account of Lot, Abraham's nephew, shows city life in a poor light, and Lot's preoccupation with cities and city dwelling runs contrapuntally through Genesis 12–19 and the story of Abraham the pilgrim promise-bearer.[15]

This attitude to cities and city building differs from that found in some Mesopotamian sources where, on the whole, the city is viewed positively. An Akkadian poem of the late second millennium which derides the city dweller as effete, incapable of showing strength or courage, is unusual for its rejection of city life.[16] A more exalted and more typical view is reflected in the Sumerian flood story, dubbed by Jacobsen 'the Eridu Genesis', according to which founding cities was a kingly responsibility:

> When the royal scepter was coming down from heaven,
> the august crown and the royal throne being already down
>   from heaven,
> he regularly performed to perfection the august divine services
>   and offices,
> laid the bricks of those cities in pure spots.[17]

---

[13] This is not just a question of addressing a rural constituency, as in the case of the Holiness Code (on which see J. Joosten, *People and Land in the Holiness Code: An Exegetical Study of the Ideational Framework of the Law in Leviticus 17–26* [SVT 67; Leiden: E.J. Brill, 1996], 155–57).

[14] See ch. 2.

[15] For discussion of cities and citizens in the prophetic books of the Old Testament see L.L. Grabbe, 'Sup-urbs or only Hyp-urbs? Prophets and Populations in Ancient Israel and Socio-historical Method', in L.L. Grabbe and R.D. Haak (eds.), *'Every City shall be Forsaken': Urbanism and Prophecy in Ancient Israel and the Near East* (SJSOT 330; Sheffield: Sheffield Academic Press, 2001), 95–123(112–21). Grabbe thinks that the city-country divide is not so sharp in the prophetic books as is sometimes imagined (121–22), and he doubts the usefulness of urbanism as an analytical tool (123).

[16] See W.W. Hallo, *Origins: The Ancient Near Eastern Background of Some Modern Western Institutions* (Studies in the History and Culture of the Ancient Near East, 6; Leiden: E.J. Brill, 1996), 2.

[17] Translation as in T. Jacobsen, 'The Eridu Genesis', *JBL* 100 (1981), 518; cf. Hallo, *Origins*, 5. Jacobsen assumes that the unpreserved beginning to the second column of the text described an unsuccessful attempt at city building (517).

The seven *apkallus* – the antediluvian sages – were credited with laying the foundations of ancient cities in Sumer.[18] According to the Epic of Gilgamesh, they were involved in the founding of Uruk.[19] Regions to the west had, of course, their own tradition of venerating city builders.[20] In Genesis, by contrast, it is more a case of the '*anti-hero*', inasmuch as it is Cain who is said to have been the founder of the first city.[21]

The question of a more general Pentateuchal reticence about Jerusalem has been addressed recently by Yairah Amit.[22] Amit does not regard historical verisimilitude – the idea that the Pentateuch respects the historical tradition that Jerusalem became part of the Israelite domain at a relatively late date – as a sufficient explanation of this reticence. She also reduces Cassuto's three claimed Pentateuchal references to Jerusalem[23] to one, and even then explains Genesis 14:18–20, where the city is thought to be indicated,[24] as an insertion, of a polemical nature, in the text.[25] She argues that there is a deliberate avoidance of the naming of Jerusalem in Deuteronomy because the Deuteronomic legislator was most interested in establishing the *principle* of cultic centralization.

---

[18] Hallo, *Origins*, 6–7. See J.C. Greenfield, 'The Seven Pillars of Wisdom (Prov. 9:1) – A Mistranslation', *JQR* 76 (1985), 13–20(16).

[19] *Gilgamesh* I:16–19(19); XI:303–305(305) (see *ANET*, 73, 97).

[20] Cf. Hallo, *Origins*, 9. See also D. Daube, 'Two Jewish Prayers', *Rechtshistorisches Journal* 6 (1987), 185–94 ('Mythology is full of rejects founding cities', 189).

[21] Hallo, *Origins*, 10, claims that the Hebrew expression used in Genesis 4:17 should be translated 'he was (or became) the builder of a city' (a few Hebrew Mss point *bnh* as a participle in the construct singular). Such a rendering may come nearer to implying that Cain was the *first* city builder.

[22] Y. Amit, *Hidden Polemics in Biblical Narrative* (tr. J. Chipman; Biblical Interpretation Series, 25; Leiden: Brill, 2000), 130–68; eadem, 'The Status of Jerusalem in the Pentateuchal Writings' (Heb.), in M. Garsiel, S. Vargon, A. Frisch, J. Kugel (eds.), *Studies in Bible and Exegesis*, 5 (Fs U. Simon; Ramat Gan: Bar Ilan University Press, 2000), 41–57. My thanks go to Professor Garsiel for drawing my attention to this article.

[23] These are Abram's encounter with Melchizedek (Gen. 14:18–20), the covenant between the pieces (Gen. 15:7–21) and the binding of Isaac (Gen. 22:1–19); see U. Cassuto, 'Jerusalem in the Pentateuch', in *Biblical and Oriental Studies*, I: *Bible* (Jerusalem: Magnes Press, 1973), 71–78; cf. Amit, *Hidden Polemics*, 136.

[24] Cf. J.A. Emerton, 'The Site of Salem, the City of Melchizedek (Genesis xiv 18)', *SVT* 41 (1990), 45–71. Emerton regards the equation of Salem with Jerusalem as 'the most probable interpretation of the available evidence' (70).

[25] *Hidden Polemics*, 157.

Developing historical circumstances made Jerusalem an uncertain prospect, and he was unwilling to tie his theology to the vagaries of history.[26] Since other anachronistic uses of place names are allowed (as in 'as far as Dan', in Gen. 14:14, though the naming of Dan is post-Pentateuchal [cf. Judg. 18:29]), and other sanctuaries are mentioned, the general Pentateuchal reticence over Jerusalem becomes the more striking.[27] The Pentateuch's silence on Jerusalem 'roars like thunder'.[28] Ultimately, says Amit, it is the Babylonian destruction of the city and its temple that has left its mark on the text in this way. The fundamentals of divine worship could not be tied to one specific place, especially one subjected to the gloomy reality of enemy invasion and destruction.

This is an interesting thesis which deserves much fuller treatment than is possible here. Amit does not refer specifically to the Primeval History, largely because the claimed references or allusions to Jerusalem with which she is concerned come after Genesis 11; but she does speak generally of 'the Torah' in connection with absent Jerusalem, and so the Primeval History may be considered to fall within the ambit of her thesis. In one important respect, her thesis might be deemed potentially more persuasive for the Pentateuch after Genesis 11, in that from chapter 12 on there is a strong interest in the land of Israel, and so references to the prospective capital city and centre of worship might naturally have been included from time to time. The patriarchs are depicted as living in the land, but, more importantly, there is a strong future orientation in the Pentateuchal references to it: the land, not yet possessed, is the promised inheritance of the descendants of the patriarchs. That being the case, there was scope for anticipatory references to Jerusalem's ultimate status, beyond the association of Abraham with Salem in Genesis 14:18–20 and with the mountain of the Lord where 'he may be seen' in Genesis 22:14.[29] Even the dictates of historical verisimilitude would have allowed such prospective references to Jerusalem. (The references to Gerizim and Shechem at sensitive points in the Samaritan Pentateuch show how even an established text tradition could be edited to serve an ideological purpose.)

---

[26] *Hidden Polemics*, 160–61.

[27] *Hidden Polemics*, 133, 139.

[28] Amit, 'The Status of Jerusalem' (Heb.), 41.

[29] Amit, *Hidden Polemics*, 149, notes that the 'mountain of the Lord' is capable of more than one interpretation, nevertheless the later the Genesis text is dated – and Amit seems no advocate of early dating for the shaping and editing of the Pentateuchal traditions generally (see *Hidden Polemics*, 165–67) – the greater the likelihood of such a term being understood of Jerusalem-Zion.

However, in the form in which Amit raises it, the issue requires a broader treatment than the mere consideration of Pentateuchal reference or non-reference to Jerusalem. For example, it would be useful to look at references to Abraham in non-Pentateuchal texts that are dated to the exilic and post-exilic periods. Among the comparatively few references to Abraham outside the Pentateuch two are from the exilic period and are appealing to his patronage, once in connection with the restoration of the ruins of Jerusalem (Isa. 51:1–3) and once in a quotation from those who believed that God had left them in charge of the ruined sites of Judah (Ezek. 33:23–26). These texts certainly do not suggest that there was a sustained attempt in the exilic period to maintain a gulf between the patriarchs and founding fathers on the one hand and Jerusalem and Judah on the other.

It remains a fact, moreover, that the Old Testament obstinately associates the annexation of Jerusalem with the reign and exploits of David. The tradition of prior Jebusite occupation and resistance until David's reign was so strong as not to be written out of the story, and it is in that respect on a par with the tradition of Israelite sojourning in Egypt: they are the kinds of traditions that are unlikely to have originated in a nation's fictionalized account of its formation and early development. This understanding of Jerusalem's prior history appears to be reflected in the rearguard position of the Jebusites in the lists of Canaanite peoples to be dispossessed in Genesis 15:21; Exodus 33:2; 34:11. It is also the case that the books of the Former Prophets are interested in the pre-Israelite history of the city (Josh. 10:1, 3, 5, 23; 12:10; 15:8, 63; 18:28; Judg. 1:7, 8, 21; 19:10; 1 Sam. 17:54), and the most natural reading of the larger picture in the Pentateuch and Former Prophets is of the maintenance of historical verisimilitude with, in the view of many scholars, some of the references in Joshua-Judges representing minor breaches of the historian's etiquette made possible by Jerusalem's supreme position in the later history of Israel and Judah.

Missing Mountains

This absence of Jerusalem from Genesis 1–11 is paralleled by an absence of mountains in the chapters about beginnings, whether as a feature of the creation in chapter 1 or of paradise in chapters 2–3.[30] This is so despite the antiquity that is generally associated with mountains in the Hebrew Bible. They have a significance that sets them

---

[30] The absence of mountains from the Genesis cosmology is noted by R.L. Cohn, *The Shape of Sacred Space: Four Biblical Studies* (American Academy of Religion Studies in Religion, 23; Chico: Scholars Press, 1981), 30.

apart from other natural features, and are regarded as belonging to the original creation. Their absence from Genesis is therefore more striking than, say, the text's failure to mention forests or lakes. This becomes all the more noticeable when Genesis 1 is put alongside Psalm 104, which is sufficiently close to the creation narrative as to have induced a 'priority wrangle' among Old Testament scholars, who find reasons for regarding the psalm as dependent on Genesis 1 or, on the other hand, as being more ancient and actually able to account for some features of the creation narrative, for example, the 'poetic' form underlying the expression 'beasts of the field' (Gen. 1:24; cf. Ps. 104:11, 20).[31] Certain elements common to the two texts, and the order in which these features are presented, would indeed suggest some kind of connection. Now, in Psalm 104 the mountains as part of the created order are mentioned half a dozen times (vv. 6, 8, 10, 13, 18, 32). Other texts speak of the antiquity of the hills: 'Were you brought forth before the hills?', asks Eliphaz of Job (Job 15:7; cf. Ps. 90:2; Prov. 8:25). Their existence is assumed, and they play a part in the flood narrative,[32] as in the Mesopotamian *Epic of Gilgamesh* where the ark comes to rest on Mount Nisir.[33] Their absence from the earlier Genesis narratives becomes still more noticeable when put against Ezekiel 28, with its hologram-like[34] presentation of the king of Tyre and the primal man, and its fusing of the paradise and mountain of God motifs:

> You were in Eden, the garden of God …
>
> You were on the holy mountain of God;
>   you walked among the fiery stones.
>
> (Ezek. 28:13, 14)

Levenson, however, does not accept the idea of a low-lying Eden, arguing that, since rivers flow downstream, Eden must be 'elevated, certainly at least a high plateau'.[35] If elevation were an issue, a relief

---

[31] Cf. J. Day, *Psalms* (Old Testament Guides; Sheffield: Sheffield Academic Press, 1990), 41–42.

[32] See Genesis 7:19–20; 8:4–5.

[33] *Gilgamesh* 11:140 (see *ANET*, 94).

[34] The term acknowledges the alternating elements in Ezekiel 28:12–19, which combines features appropriate respectively to the primal man and the king of Tyre.

[35] *Sinai and Zion*, 129. W. Zimmerli, *Ezechiel*, 2: *Ezechiel 25–48* (BKAT 13/2; Neukirchen-Vluyn: Neukirchener Verlag, 1969), 1192, thinks that a high mountain is indicated in the reference to Eden in Genesis 2:10–14, seeing that all the rivers of the primeval world derive from there. See also M. Fishbane, *Text and Texture: Close Readings of Selected Biblical Texts* (New York: Schocken, 1979), 112.

from the palace of Ashurbanipal in Nineveh shows how the necessary arrangements could be conceived in Assyria. The relief depicts a temple atop a mountain, and a tree-filled garden that is irrigated by a river and its distributaries.[36] The river is conveyed to the elevation on which the temple stands by means of an aqueduct. There is no particular reason, however, to think of Eden as high ground. In a discussion of this sort we should also have to take into account possible derivations of the name 'Eden', which, according to one explanation, is connected with the Sumero-Akkadian *edin(u)*, meaning 'steppe' or 'plain'.[37] The basis of this etymology has, however, been seriously questioned.[38] Others have accepted that Genesis 1(2)–3 not only mentions no mountains but assumes no mountains, in this respect merely reflecting the lowland Mesopotamian background of the tradition (cf. Gen. 2:8, 'a garden in the east').[39] This would not be so easy to sustain within the context of a source-critical analysis of the chapters, since two sources have traditionally been recognized, both are deficient in mountain references, and the case for thinking that both originated in Mesopotamia would need demonstrating. One way and another, whatever we may have to assume or presuppose for Genesis 1–3, the creation and Eden traditions are surprisingly silent about mountains, holy or otherwise.

So is it just coincidence that Genesis 1–3 omits mountains? Or is the absence to be explained by an aversion to the idea of the 'sacred mountain' because of its non-Israelite associations, and despite the prospering of the Zion mountain tradition in other parts of the Old Testament? The Babel tower of Genesis 11:1–9 is sometimes viewed as an artificial mountain, but, even though

---

[36] See O. Keel, *The Symbolism of the Biblical World: Ancient Near Eastern Iconography and the Book of Psalms* (tr. T.J. Hallett; New York: Seabury Press, 1978), 150 (no. 202), 396.

[37] Cf. E.A. Speiser, *Genesis* (AB 1; Garden City: Doubleday, 1964), 16.

[38] See D.T. Tsumura, *The Earth and the Waters in Genesis 1 and 2: A Linguistic Investigation* (SJSOT 83; Sheffield: JSOT Press, 1989), 123–37 ('Etymology of Eden' [123–25 on Sumerian *edin*, Akkadian *edinu*]). Tsumura thinks that the name signifies a place of plentiful water (136–37). Cf. A.R. Millard and P. Bordreuil, who suggest an association with the root *'dn*, implying 'fertility', as it appears in the Old Aramaic text in the Tell Fekhariyeh inscriptions ('A Statue from Syria with Assyrian and Aramaic Inscriptions', *BA* 45 [1982], 135–41[140, lines 4–5]); A. Abou-Assaf, P. Bordreuil, A.R. Millard, *La Statue de Tell Fekherye et son inscription bilingue assyro-araméenne* (Études Assyriologiques, 7; Paris: Éditions Recherche sur les Civilisations, 1982), 30.

[39] So R.L. Cohn, 'The Mountains and Mount Zion', *Judaism* 26 (1977), 97–115(101).

the negative casting of this 'mountain' would chime in with our theme of the absentee mountain in chapters 1–3, this explanation of the tower is too precarious to be pressed. The Mesopotamian ziggurat, as a kind of artificial mountain, may lie in the background of the Genesis story, but nothing is made there of the Babel tower other than as a primitive skyscraper. Whatever the reason, we have no Zion and no mountains in Genesis 1–3.

A Wider Purview

However we explain the near-total absence of Jerusalem from Genesis and the Pentateuch generally – and even if we do not regard it as an issue – the fact remains that Genesis 1–11 moves only slowly in the direction of the ancestors of Israel and, initially, is concerned not with the making of Israel-Judah but with the creation of the heavens and the earth and with the whole human family. This Israelite self-exclusion from the account of beginnings is striking, corresponding in a fashion to the biblical tradition of the non-autochthonous origins of Israel. For if autochthony (or 'indigenousness') was 'the noblest origin in the eyes of the Greeks', the natural tendency of any people would be to regard itself as having always been resident in its territory, unless historical memory dictated otherwise.[40] Moreover, when finally the focus is narrowed to Abraham, the talk is of God's blessing the nations through him (Gen. 12:3; 18:18; 22:18; cf. 17:4–5 ['father of many nations']; 26:4–5 [Isaac]). The universal dimension in the Primeval History is noted by T.L. Thompson in his book *The Bible in History*. While making the questionable claim that Israel is in some sense autochthonous in Genesis 1–11 – that is, is represented as belonging originally in the land in which the narrative action is taking place[41] – Thompson rightly

---

[40] Cf. J.M. Scott, *Geography in Early Judaism and Christianity: The Book of Jubilees* (SNTSMS 113; Cambridge: Cambridge University Press, 2002), 196n. 54. D. Damrosch, *The Narrative Covenant: Transformations of Genre in the Growth of Biblical Literature* (San Francisco: Harper & Row, 1987), 44, suggests that, in the confessional statement in Deuteronomy 26:5–10, 'the Deuteronomists portray their genuinely young culture as much younger than it really was', although it is not clear how serious a statement about 'origins' as such is being offered in the biblical text.

[41] *The Bible in History*, 39. Thompson refers particularly to Genesis 10–11 in this connection.

observes that Genesis starts from the perspective of the unity of mankind, and that its interest is always broader than that of Israel alone.[42] This range of interest he attributes to Hellenism's 'belief in the common origin and universal quality of humanity, in spite of its obvious diversity'.[43]

The attribution of Genesis 1–11 to Hellenistic circles of tradition makers is not ground that many Old Testament specialists share with Thompson. Nevertheless, we can, at the least, pause with him to note the wide range of interest and the partial self-exclusion that are features of Israel's account of primeval times. They are also features of the Old Testament more generally, and ones which, alongside the particularities of Israelite belief and practice, surprise us again and again as we read of the place and the prospects of the non-Jewish nations in the world that God was expected to bring into being.

I conclude, then, that the silence of Genesis 1–11 on Jerusalem arises in the first instance from a recognition of the claims of historical veracity. Jerusalem is not mentioned because it was not believed to have played a part in the world's earliest history. In practice, if not by design, this stands in contrast with the ideologically loaded account of the origins of Babylon, which, as we have noted, are associated in one influential creation account with the creation itself. Babylon-Babel does feature in Genesis, but late in the day of 'beginnings', and as the butt of a biblical satire that dismisses the best efforts of the imperial enemy as nothing more than hollow human pretension. Those later rabbinic texts that sought to honour Jerusalem by securing it a place at creation were themselves introducing something that may have been consciously omitted from the Genesis account of beginnings.

However, although there is no writing of Jerusalem/Zion back into Genesis 1–11, our next chapter shows that the 'Protohistory' does make use of the concepts of sanctuary and holy land in its accounts of the first humans.

---

[42] *The Bible in History*, 89. Cf. P. Machinist, 'The Question of Distinctiveness in Ancient Israel: An Essay', in M. Cogan and I. Eph'al (eds.), *Ah, Assyria...Studies in Assyrian History and Ancient Near Eastern Historiography Presented to Hayim Tadmor* (=*Scripta Hierosolymitana*, 33; Jerusalem: Magnes Press, 1991): 'Cosmogony where it occurs in the Biblical text is not identical with national history. Similarly, there is no notion of autochthonous origins ... of a primordial connection between the people and a particular territory' (208); 'In Egypt, we find no such assertions; the history of nation and the cities within was understood as coterminous with cosmogony' (209).

[43] *The Bible in History*, 40.

Chapter Two

The Land Theology of Genesis 4

The absence of explicit reference to Jerusalem in Genesis 1–3, or for that matter Genesis 1–11, does not mean that the 'Primeval History' could completely divest itself of Hebrew thought categories any more than it could dispense with the Hebrew language in which it is written. If, for example, the heavenly lights of Genesis 1:14 are 'for signs and *festivals*',[1] and not just 'for signs and seasons', it is hardly non-Israelite festivals that are in view.[2] The more substantial case of retrojection to which we now turn also relates to the cult, for a number of modern writers on Genesis have endorsed the view, already represented in ancient sources, that echoes of the temple-tabernacle traditions are present in the creation and Eden narratives.[3] Thus, if we take Genesis 1:1–2:4a, it has been claimed that in this account the whole cosmos has been constructed so as to function as the residence of the divine creator. The idea is expressed by Philo of

---

[1] The 'sacred seasons' explanation is described as 'most probable' in *BDB*, 417; cf. *HALAT*, 2, 529.

[2] Since we are now in the area of religious observance, such a momentary piece of 'particularity' is quite compatible with other, more universal, strains noted for Genesis 1 in the previous chapter.

[3] Levenson, *Sinai and Zion: An Entry into the Jewish Bible* (Minneapolis: Winston Press, 1985), 142–45; G.J. Wenham, *Genesis 1–15* (WBC 1; Waco: Word Books, 1987), 65, 67; E.E. Elnes, 'Creation and Tabernacle: The Priestly Writer's "Environmentalism"', *Horizons in Biblical Theology* 16 (1994), 144–55(147–53); T.D. Alexander, 'Beyond Borders: The Wider Dimensions of Land', in P.S. Johnston and P.W.L. Walker (eds.), *The Land of Promise: Biblical, Theological and Contemporary Perspectives* (Leicester: Apollos, 2000), 35–50(40–41). Cf. Jubilees 3:8–14 (where the post-partum laws of Leviticus 12:1–5 are applied to Eden); 8:19; 4QSerekh Damascus Document (4Q265), fr. 7, col. 2, lines 11–17. Already there is conflation of paradise and holy mount traditions in Isaiah 11:1–9; 65:23–25.

Alexandria,[4] though he does not refer specifically to Genesis in this connection.[5]

The verbal parallels between the accounts of the inspection of the finished creation and the completed tabernacle (see Gen. 1:22, 28, 31; 2:1, 3; Exod. 39:32, 43) have been especially influential with modern writers. However, in this case I am inclined to agree with Hurowitz that these particular parallels arise because the work of creation, like the construction of the tabernacle, is being described as if it is a building operation.[6] God and Moses are fulfilling the role of building inspectors, pronouncing blessings and thus expressing their approval of the respective edifices:

God blessed them, saying ...

(Gen. 1:22 [cf. 1:28; 2:3])

God saw all that he had made ...

(Gen. 1:31)

The heavens and earth and all their array were completed.

(Gen. 2:1)

On the seventh day God completed his work that he had been doing.

(Gen. 2:2)

Moses saw all the work ... and Moses blessed them.

(Exod. 39:43)

All the work of the tabernacle of the tent of meeting was completed.

(Exod. 39:32)

---

[4] 'The highest, and in truth the holy, temple of God is, as we must acknowledge, the whole universe ...' (*De Specialibus Legibus* 1:66). For the view that the creation-tabernacle parallels are intended to suggest the participation of Israel in the completion of God's creative activity see M. Fishbane, *Text and Texture: Close Readings of Selected Biblical Texts* (New York: Schocken, 1979), 12–13.

[5] Cf. S. Dean McBride, 'Divine Protocol: Genesis 1:1–2:3 as Prologue to the Pentateuch', in W.P. Brown and S.D. McBride (eds.), *God Who Creates: Essays in Honor of W. Sibley Towner* (Grand Rapids: Eerdmans, 2000), 3–41(11n. 21).

[6] V. Hurowitz, *I Have Built You an Exalted House: Temple Building in the Bible in Light of Mesopotamian and Northwest Semitic Writings* (SJSOT 115; JSOT/ASOR Monograph Series, 5; Sheffield: Sheffield Academic Press, 1992), 242.

In the Eden narrative in Genesis 2–3, precious stones (2:12) and cherubim (3:24) are among the more obvious features shared with the tabernacle and temple.[7] The tree of life also has its counterpart in the stylized tree of the menorah that stood in the outer compartment of the tabernacle (Exod. 25:31–40).

Tabernacle parallels apart, it is sometimes suggested that Eden is the permanent dwelling-place of God in Genesis 2–3.[8] Noticeably, there is no language of divine 'descent' in the narrative: it could be inferred that God resided in Eden. We may recall in this connection that it was at the sources of 'the two [subterranean] rivers' that the Canaanite high god El had his abode,[9] and that the biblical paradise was furnished with a river (2:10). So, at a crucial point, Adam and Eve simply hear the sound of the Lord God walking in the garden in the cool of the day (3:8), as if he has been somewhere in the vicinity all the time. However, this notion of Eden as permanent divine abode probably assumes too much about a text that shows the garden in the making, and that would most naturally be taken to imply that the divine landscaper had some other abode independent of his new venture. Indeed, Stordalen has concluded from his study of the significance of the garden in the ancient near east that it does not normally function as a divine residence; gods generally prefer structured dwellings.[10] Moreover, the emphasis in Genesis 3 is on denial of access to the tree of life rather than on the primal couple's unfitness for the dwelling-place of God (see 3:22, 24). Evidently their prior nakedness was not considered an affront to the divine presence (2:25), as it would have been in the historical period, which knows a prohibition on nakedness for priests engaging in altar service (Exod. 20:26; cf. Gen. 3:7). In the end, it may be, as

---

[7] Wenham, *Genesis 1–15*, 65, 86; idem, 'Sanctuary Symbolism in the Garden of Eden Story', *Proceedings of the World Congress of Jewish Studies*, 9 (1986), 19–25; K.A. Mathews, *Genesis 1–11:26* (The New American Commentary, 1A; npl: Broadman and Holman, 1996), 52, 255. J.P. Schultz, 'From Sacred Space to Sacred Object to Sacred Person in Jewish Antiquity', *Shofar* 12 (1993), 28–37, notes the connection between creation and temple in Psalm 24 – an association that does not require composite authorship for explanation (31–32).

[8] Cf. H.N. Wallace, *The Eden Narrative* (Harvard Semitic Monographs, 32; Atlanta: Scholars Press, 1985), 80.

[9] Cf. M.H. Pope, *El in the Ugaritic Texts* (SVT 2; Leiden: E.J. Brill, 1955), 61–81.

[10] T. Stordalen, *Echoes of Eden: Genesis 2–3 and Symbolism of the Eden Garden in Biblical Hebrew Literature* (Contributions to Biblical Exegesis and Theology, 25; Leuven: Peeters, 2000), 139–61(157–60), 298.

White suggests,[11] that God's walking in the garden in Genesis 3:8 is to be seen as a narrative device, to bring God more directly – we might say, confrontationally – into the action, as compared with his previous speaking role in the narrative (cf. 2:16–17, 18). Thus, although Eden may be regarded as having sanctuary features, it does not follow that it is depicted as the permanent home of God, any more than the tabernacle and temple traditions necessarily represent a limiting of the abode of God to an earthly shrine.[12]

The Holy Land

If Genesis 2–3 sees the primal couple ejected from an Eden-sanctuary, chapter 4 seems to take this idea a stage further with the expulsion of Cain from 'holy land'. The chapter begins with Cain and Abel on the outside of Eden and engaged with the matter of approach, by means of sacrifice, to God. For, while 3:24 talks of the banishment of Adam and Eve from Eden, the situation at the beginning of chapter 4 is not that of total exclusion, of them or their offspring, from the divine presence. However, Cain comes under a divine curse for having killed his brother, and the accompanying sentence contains more than a hint of the land theology of other parts of the Hebrew canon where the land is viewed as experiencing the divine presence in a unique manner, and is at the same time understood to have been gifted by God to Israel. The familiar term 'holy land' satisfactorily describes this situation. As Joosten has shown, Old Testament texts sometimes envisage the Jerusalem sanctuary and the land of Israel as coterminous, so that the land is 'holy' in the strictest sense.[13] In the so-called 'Holiness Code' (Lev. 17–26), on the other hand, the finer nuances of the semantic field of holiness are observed, and there the land is regarded as 'pure' rather than 'holy' (cf. Lev. 18:24–28). Here the expression 'holy land' is

---

[11] H.C. White, *Narration and Discourse in the Book of Genesis* (Cambridge: Cambridge University Press, 1991), 138: 'The narrative has now produced two alienated realms of characters ... God and the humans must then become external objects to each other ... God must *act* to restore direct communication; he needs to acquire position in the narrative for the first time.'

[12] Stordalen, *Echoes of Eden*, 298, speaks of Eden as 'pointing to a *mediated* presence of YHWH God'. This derives from his conclusion, on the basis of biblical and other evidence, that gardens 'manifest divine forces'.

[13] J. Joosten, *People and Land in the Holiness Code: An Exegetical Study of the Ideational Framework of the Law in Leviticus 17–26* (SVT 67; Leiden: E.J. Brill, 1996), 178–80.

retained as implying a special status which, in the nature of the case, probably cannot be defined more closely.[14]

There may be a hint of land theology already in Genesis 4:11, in the sentence formally pronounced on Cain: 'Now you are cursed from the ground'.[15] The wording recalls the judgment on the serpent in 3:14, 'You are cursed more than all the livestock'. However, a formally parallel translation such as, 'Now you are cursed more than the ground' seems very unlikely. Cain's alienation from the ground that was meant to sustain him appears to be in view here in 4:11. *NIV*, assuming heavy pregnancy in the Hebrew original, has, 'Now you are under a curse and driven from the ground ...'[16] The idea becomes more explicit in 4:14, where Cain protests that, in 'driving' him from the land, God is banishing him from his presence. The operative verb is *g-r-š* as in 3:24, where it is used to describe the banishment of Adam and Eve from Eden. This makes explicit the comparison between Cain's 'expulsion' and that of Adam and Eve,[17] with the proviso that Cain's marks a further step away from the divine presence as originally experienced in the garden.[18] Many of the occurrences of *g-r-š* ('drive out') in the rest of the Old Testament relate to the expulsion of the Canaanite inhabitants of the land prior to the Israelite 'settlement' (e.g. Exod. 23:28, 31; 34:11). So it appears that, however one translates 4:14,[19] the verse takes us in the direction of 'land theology'. When, according to verse 16, Cain 'went out from the Lord's presence', this marks the end of his audience with God,[20] but in the context it may also

---

[14] Cf. M. Weinfeld, *The Promise of the Land: The Inheritance of the Land of Canaan by the Israelites* (The Taubman Lectures in Jewish Studies, 3; Berkeley: University of California Press, 1993), 219–21.

[15] U. Cassuto relates the curse to Abel's vengeance-seeking blood, calling out from the ground, in verse 10 (*A Commentary on the Book of Genesis* [Heb.] [5th edn; Jerusalem: Magnes Press, 1969], 147). The Masoretic punctuation makes the major break in the sentence after 'Now you are cursed', in which case the preposition *min* may have to be rendered 'because of'.

[16] Cf. *REB* 'Now you are accursed and will be banished from the very ground.'

[17] On points of parallel between Genesis 3 and 4 see Mathews, *Genesis 1–11:26*, 263.

[18] Cf. Wenham, *Genesis 1–15*, 100, 108 ('There is development: sin is more firmly entrenched and humanity is further alienated from God' [100]).

[19] *RV* '[T]hou hast driven me out this day from the face of the ground'; *NEB* '[T]hou hast driven me today from the ground'; *NIV* 'Today you are driving me from the land'.

[20] Cf. D. Daube, 'Two Jewish Prayers', *Rechtshistorisches Journal* 6 (1987), 185–94(189), who cites the 'courtly formula' of Genesis 41:46; 47:10; Exodus 35:20.

suggest his removal of himself from the land of the divine presence. Cain's crime and his fate are to some degree paralleled in the story of Absalom, whose flight to Geshur after his murder of Amnon (2 Sam. 13:38) was a self-imposed expulsion from the land (cf. 2 Sam. 14:13[14]).

In Genesis 3–4, then, the distancing of the first humans from God occurs in two stages, and there appears to be reflected in the accounts something of the (mainly) priestly conceptuality of 'graded holiness'[21] and, in one or other sense of the term, 'Sacred Geography'[22]:

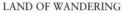

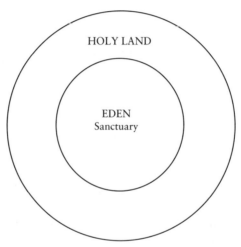

That Genesis 4 invokes 'holy land' ideology is supported by a comparison with 1 Samuel 26:19–20 where David, about to become a fugitive from the murderous envy of Saul, complains to Saul that he is driving him out from his share in 'the heritage of the Lord', that is, beyond the borders of Israel.

---

[21] Cf. the use of the term 'graded holiness' in the monograph by P.P. Jenson (*Graded Holiness: A Key to the Priestly Conception of the World* [SJSOT 106; Sheffield: JSOT Press, 1992], esp. 36–38).

[22] For thoroughgoing 'graded holiness', progressing out from the 'holy of holies' to the sanctuary, the city and the land, in the Qumran Temple Scroll (11QT), see H. Lichtenberger, '"Im Lande Israel zu wohnen wiegt alle Gebote der Tora auf." Die Heiligkeit des Landes und die Heiligung des Lebens', in R. Feldmeier and U. Heckel (eds.), *Die Heiden: Juden, Christen und das Problem des Fremden* (WUNT 70; Tübingen: J.C.B. Mohr [Paul Siebeck], 1994), 92–107(94–96).

> You have driven me out this day from the face of the ground, and I shall
> be hidden from your presence ... whoever finds me will kill me.
>
> (Gen. 4:14–15)

> [T]hey have driven me out this day that I should have no share in the
> heritage of the Lord ... let not my blood fall to the earth away from
> the presence of the Lord.
>
> (1 Sam. 26:19–20)

In both Genesis 4:14 and 1 Samuel 26:19 it is the verb *g-r-š* that is
used for the act of expulsion, and there is the further parallel that
both Cain and David speak of it as taking place 'today'. This time-
reference formalizes the occasion or event – DeVries uses the term
'epitomizing'[23] – in the way of a number of its other Old Testament
occurrences (cf. Gen. 41:41[LXX]; 47:23; Exod. 32:29; 1 Sam.
15:28; Ps. 2:7; Ruth 4:9–10).[24] In addition, David expresses a Cain-
like anxiety lest his blood should fall to the ground away from the
presence of the Lord (v. 20; cf. Gen. 4:14–15).

The underlying idea in 1 Samuel 26:19–20 is that of Israel as the
'holy land' where God's presence is experienced; to go beyond its
borders is to forfeit the protection of that presence. For its part, even
though Genesis 4 is dealing with primeval times, it can still invoke
the concept of the 'holy land', with the ground (*'dmh*) whence Cain
is banished taking on the significance of the *'dmt hqdš* ('holy land')
of Zechariah 2:16 (cf. *gbwl qdšw*, Ps. 78:54).[25] It is clear, therefore,
that interpretations of Genesis 4 in terms of Cain's alienation from
human society, or of his expulsion because the ground was defiled
by Abel's blood, must also take the broader concept of 'land theology' into account. In other words, just as Cain became in the post-
biblical period a *topos* for Sadducean-type rejection of belief in
afterlife and human accountability – witness, for example, the
Targum insertions in Genesis 4:8, supplying what the Hebrew text
was thought to have lost[26] – so already in the biblical text he is an
expellee from the 'holy land', and the first biblical 'exile'.

---

[23] S.J. DeVries, *Yesterday, Today and Tomorrow: Time and History in the
Old Testament* (Grand Rapids: Eerdmans, 1975), 139–277.
[24] Cf., on the expression as formalizing legal terminology, G.M. Tucker,
'Witnesses and "Dates" in Israelite Contracts', *CBQ* 28 (1966), 42–45.
[25] Weinfeld, *The Promise of the Land*, 203, denies that there is a 'holy land'
concept in the Old Testament. In Zechariah 2:16(12) the expression is
thought to refer to 'the Temple and Temple city'. However, if the term is
limited in this way it fits its context less readily.
[26] See R.P. Gordon, 'The Targumists as Eschatologists', *SVT* 29 (1978),
113–30(126–29).

In a sense, therefore, it is not merely the *ground* that is polluted by the shedding of Abel's blood but *the land*, to the extent that the later concept is influential in the telling of Cain's story. The idea of 'holy land' and of ejection from it is expressed with peculiar force in Leviticus 18:28, in a text falling within the 'Holiness Code': 'lest the land vomit you out, when you defile it, just as it vomited out the nation that was before you'.[27] The ultimate justification for viewing Israel as the 'holy' or 'pure' land was, as we have noted, the belief that God himself resided in it ('You shall not defile the land in which you live, in the midst of which I reside', Num. 35:34; cf. Josh. 22:19).[28] It is an idea more formative in Genesis 4 than in Genesis 3, for, although Eden has sanctuary-type features, we have observed that the emphasis in that chapter is not so much on banishment from sacred territory as on denial of access to the tree of life, in ful-filment of the original warning to the primal man that to eat from the forbidden tree would mean immediate loss of life (2:17).

The First City

In strict chronological terms the 'holy land' of Israel is far from view in Genesis 4, yet the concept is invoked in the telling of the story of Cain's rejection by God. As Genesis 4 proceeds, Cain builds a city somewhere in the land of 'wandering' (v. 16) and calls it after his son Enoch (4:17). This is, on the face of it, a contradiction of his sentence to a life of rest-less wandering outside 'the land', and that is precisely the point. There is no need to resort to anthropology and wandering tinkers settling down in city life in order to explain Cain's city building.[29] Nor should the source criticism of Genesis 4 be influenced by this apparent irrec-oncilability between Cain's judgment and his response to it.[30] Nor need we force the Hebrew to say that it was, in fact, Cain's son Enoch who built the city, though a number of writers prefer to construe the text in this way.[31]

---

[27] Cf. White, *Narration and Discourse*, 164.

[28] Cf. Joosten, *People and Land in the Holiness Code*, 178–80.

[29] So G. von Rad, *Genesis: A Commentary* (Old Testament Library; revd edn; London: SCM Press, 1972), 110.

[30] Some writers invoke separate sources to explain the apparent discordance between Cain's sentence and his city building (e.g. W.H. Bennett, *Genesis* [Century Bible; London: Caxton, nd], 120).

[31] Cf. Wenham, *Genesis 1–15*, 111 ('the supposition that Cain built the first city comes, strangely, after his condemnation to a wandering life in the immediately preceding verses'); cf. R.W.L. Moberly, reviewing R.S. Hendel, *The Text of Genesis 1–11: Textual Studies and Critical Edition* (1998), in *JTS* NS 51 (2000), 188–90(189), noting also the possibility that 'city' ('*yr*)

The attraction of making Cain's son the builder of the first city mentioned in the Bible is that if Enoch, whose name comes as the last word in the Hebrew of verse 17, is made the subject of the verb 'build', then Enoch may be said to have called the city (ᶜyr) after his son Irad (ᶜyrd). This produces paronomasia of a sort, if we assume that the city was simply called 'City' (ᶜyr). The suggestion is attractive, and the wordplay would be on a level with actual occurrences of such namings in Genesis (e.g. the linking of the city of Babel with the Hebrew verb *bālal* ['confuse'] in 11:9), yet the explanation of Enoch as the subject of 'built' and 'called' despite the rearguard position of the name within verse 17 is unconvincing. Cassuto argued that the comparable construction used in 4:2 in connection with Abel shows that Enoch must be the subject of 'called' in verse 17,[32] but the repetition of Abel's name before the verb in verse 2b makes an important difference. If anything, 4:2 shows that, when the object of the verb in one clause ('gave birth to Abel') is to become the subject in the next ('Abel was a shepherd'), the word should be repeated before the verb in the second clause.[33] Moreover, if the city was named after Irad, we might have expected the reference to Enoch's building and naming of it to occur in verse 18, after the report of Irad's birth.[34]

In the end, the decision is not so crucial as it may appear. Even if the builder of the city was Cain's son, the idea of resistance against a sentence to nomady can still be present, by dint of Enoch's relation to Cain. This, after all, is how the 'sinful culture' of Genesis 4:20–22 is often explained: the brief account of early human 'progress'

---

[31] (*continued*) may be named after Enoch's son Irad, if Enoch rather than Cain is the builder.

[32] Cassuto, *Commentary on the Book of Genesis*, 154–55.

[33] The question may be complicated by the contrasting mentions of Abel and Cain in verse 2b.

[34] The identity of the builder might be settled if we admitted the typological argument considered by Weinfeld, according to which Cain would have 'set out' and then built and named the city, just as it is reported of Nimrod in Genesis 10:11 that he 'went out to Assyria and built Nineveh, Rehovoth-Ir and Calah' (cf. Mic. 5:5[6]) (*The Promise of the Land*, 18–19). However, in Genesis 4:16 Cain 'went out from the Lord's presence and lived in the land of Nod to the east of Eden'. The going out is not linked directly with the building of the city, as in Genesis 10. It may be that the MT in 4:17 means something like 'became the builder of (cf. Heb. Mss) a city' and presents Cain/Enoch as more of a founding father in relation to city building (such language is used in vv. 20 and 21 of tent dwelling and music making). *NIV* 'Cain was then building' overlooks this possible nuance.

introduced in these verses is tied to the line of Cain and suffers by association. It could also be the case with the Cainite city, even if the builder was Enoch. Nothing is otherwise said of the significance of this city. It has no religious associations, and no sanctuary function such as is attributed to the earliest cities of Sumer, as in the following quotation from a tablet found at Nippur and dating to the Old Babylonian period:

> May they come and build cities and cult-places,
>   that I may cool myself in their shade;
> may they lay the bricks for the cult-cities
>   in pure spots, and
> may they found places for divination
>   in pure spots.[35]

In Genesis 4, it is with the birth of Seth's son Enosh that the worship of God truly begins (4:26): 'then people began to call on the name of the Lord'.

Cain is depicted as a man in basic contention with God, as is illustrated by his responses to God (e.g. vv. 9, 14). In purely social terms, his crime of fratricide is much more serious than the sin of Adam and Eve. It is, then, very much in keeping with his portrayal that he is sentenced to lifelong wandering and responds by building a city.[36] The entrance of murder into the human story in Genesis 4 rather than Genesis 3 might, of course, be said to have good casting reasons behind it. To emphasize the enormity of Cain's murder of Abel over against the petty disobedience of Adam and Eve, perhaps with the thought of relativizing the importance of the 'Fall' narrative in chapter 3, overlooks the point that, if Cain's crime were transferred to one of the human protagonists in chapter 3, there would be no human story to be told.

The story of Cain is told, then, partly in terms of the holy land concept as it developed within the biblical tradition. However, just as our opening chapter showed that early Genesis denies Jerusalem/Zion a mythological presence in its account of beginnings, so our next will consider a couple of ways in which the biblical writers' portrayal of the city in the historical period differs from other ancient 'city-talk'.

---

[35] Translation as in T. Jacobsen, 'The Eridu Genesis', *JBL* 100 (1981), 513–29(515).

[36] Cf. Daube, 'Two Jewish Prayers', 189.

Chapter Three

The City of God

Once it became recognized as Israel's cultic centre, Jerusalem assumed in the biblical tradition a unique status that it has never since lost. That meant that there were special ways of talking about it, and ways in which biblical writers did not talk about it. However, as we shall see, in the case of omphalos mythology post-biblical writers were quite happy to hitch the 'holy city' to a Greek chariot.

The God of Jerusalem

The link between the God of Israel and Jerusalem – or Zion, as it is often called in the Psalms and prophets – is represented in various titles and expressions in the Old Testament. Zion is 'the city of God' (Pss. 46:4; 87:3), 'the city of the Lord of hosts' (Ps. 48:8), 'the city of the Lord' (Ps. 101:8), to go no further than the Psalter. By contrast, expressions of the sort 'the God of Zion' or 'the God of Jerusalem' are almost completely absent from the Old Testament. There is an exception in 2 Chronicles 32:19, where Sennacherib's officers 'spoke about the God of Jerusalem as they did about the gods of the peoples of the world – the work of human hands'. Here, then, the term is associated with Assyrian ridicule of Israel's God. 2 Kings does not have a directly parallel passage, but, in a comparable utterance from the Assyrian side, several Syrian city states are the butt of the same kind of ridicule: 'Where are the gods of Hamath and Arpad? Where are the gods of Sepharvaim, Hena and Ivvah? Have they rescued Samaria from my hand?' (2 Kgs. 18:34). The title 'God of Jerusalem' occurs in Aramaic form in Ezra 7:19, in the text of the letter from Artaxerxes to Ezra authorizing his return to Jerusalem: 'Deliver before the God of Jerusalem the vessels that are given to you for the service of the house of your God.' The expression 'the God who is in Jerusalem' occurs in Ezra 1:3, in the decree of the Persian monarch Cyrus permitting the return of diaspora Jews to Jerusalem. While this expression falls short of being a formal title, it is noticeably, again, associated with a non-Israelite who would have been more at home with the concept of the 'city god'.[1] For this reason, it is not certain that the term 'God of Jerusalem' in 2 Chronicles 32:19 is the Chronicler's own coinage, as if by this means he is opposing Israel's God to the city gods mentioned in the parallel text at 2 Kings 18:34 but not named in his own summary of what Sennacherib's officers said.[2] Even if the title is the Chronicler's own invention, he may have used it because this was how a non-Israelite might speak of the God worshipped in the chief city of Judah.

A possible extra-biblical occurrence of the title 'God of Jerusalem' has been identified in the Khirbet Beit Lei tomb inscriptions discovered in 1961 about eight kilometres east of Lachish. These graffiti, which appear to be unrelated to the burials in the cave where they were found, are very difficult to read, so that although both Naveh[3] and Lemaire[4] find the title in the upper inscription of the antechamber ('YHWH is the God of all the earth; the mountains of Judah belong to the God of Jerusalem' [Naveh; cf. Lemaire]), Zevit's more recent re-evaluation shows how insecure this reading is.[5]

This near-total absence from the Old Testament of titles such as 'God of Zion' and 'God of Jerusalem' may not be accidental. In this way, any appearance of relegating Israel's God to the status of a city god, like so many of the deities of the ancient near east, is avoided.[6] City gods, and titles of the sort 'god of Ekron' (cf. 2 Kgs. 1:2), were commonplace in the surrounding cultures. The gods themselves could become fronts for inter-city politics: earthbound city rivalries

---

[1] The expression should also be read in the light of the designation of the Judahites' God as 'the Lord, the God of heaven' (v. 2) and 'the Lord, the God of Israel' (v. 3).

[2] On this possibility see P. Beentjes, 'Jerusalem in the Book of Chronicles', in M. Poorthuis and Ch. Safrai (eds.), *The Centrality of Jerusalem: Historical Perspectives* (Kampen: Kok Pharos, 1996), 15–28(27–28).

[3] J. Naveh, 'Old Hebrew Inscriptions in a Burial Cave', *IEJ* 13 (1963), 74–92(84–85, 90–92). Naveh thinks that the inscription may reflect circumstances in which Judean control was limited to Jerusalem at the time of Sennacherib's attack in 701 BC (91–92).

[4] A. Lemaire, 'Prières en temps de crise: les inscriptions de Khirbet Beit Lei', *RB* 83 (1976), 558–68(558–60).

[5] Z. Zevit, *The Religions of Ancient Israel: A Synthesis of Parallactic Approaches* (London: Continuum, 2001), 405–38(422–23).

[6] For illustration of the 'deified city' in Mesopotamia see M. Nissinen, 'City as Lofty as Heaven: Arbela and Other Cities in Neo-Assyrian Prophecy', in L.L. Grabbe and R.D. Haak (eds.), *'Every City shall be Forsaken': Urbanism and Prophecy in Ancient Israel and the Near East* (SJSOT 330; Sheffield: Sheffield Academic Press, 2001), 172–209(177–78).

could be projected on to the representative deities in the higher realms.[7] When, on the other hand, a title like 'God of Bethel' is accepted in the Old Testament, a special point is being made about the nature of the relationship between, in this case, God and the patriarch Jacob, who had encountered God in a life-challenging way on his previous visit to Bethel (Gen. 31:13; cf. 28:10–22).[8] At the same time, God is associated with the people and land of Israel in the expression 'God of Israel' in various Old Testament texts. This naturally represents a claim to rather more than the chief city of Israel as the domain of Israel's God.

As the Kuntillet ᶜAjrud inscriptions show, outside the Old Testament even the divine name itself could be attached to a city name, as in 'YHWH of Samaria' and 'YHWH of Teman'.[9] It has been suggested that a similar usage is to be found at 2 Samuel 15:7, where Absalom is supposed to have made a vow to 'YHWH-in-Hebron', which expression would represent a particular cult of YHWH associated with Hebron.[10] The more natural sense of the verse is, however, that Absalom claimed that, while he was exiled in Aram, he vowed to God that, if he returned safely to Jerusalem, he would go to Hebron to worship the Lord. More to the point, he probably reckoned that Hebron was the most suitable rallying-place for those sympathetic to his cause (cf. 2 Sam. 15:10).

---

[7] Cf. T. Jacobsen, *Kingship and the Gods: A Study of Ancient Near Eastern Religion as the Integration of Society and Nature* (Chicago: University of Chicago Press, 1948), 242.

[8] 'God of Bethel' seems to be the appropriate translation of MT *ha'el beth-'el* in Genesis 31:13.

[9] Cf. J.A. Emerton, 'New Light on Israelite Religion: The Implications of the Inscriptions from Kuntillet Ajrud', *ZAW* 94 (1982), 2–20; J.M. Hadley, *The Cult of Asherah in Ancient Israel and Judah: Evidence for a Hebrew Goddess* (University of Cambridge Oriental Publications, 57; Cambridge: Cambridge University Press, 2000), 121–29.

[10] Cf. P.R. Ackroyd, *The Second Book of Samuel* (The Cambridge Bible Commentary; Cambridge: Cambridge University Press, 1977), 138–39. A. Biran, 'To the God who is in Dan', in A. Biran (ed.), *Temples and High Places in Biblical Times* (Jerusalem: Hebrew Union College-Jewish Institute of Religion, 1981), 142–51, discusses a bilingual (Greek-Aramaic) dedicatory inscription from the late third or second century BC which may have the expression 'the God who is in Dan' ('To the God/who is in Dan/Zoilos made a vow'). However, the Greek *en Danois* may more probably mean 'among the Danites' (cf. the comment by D. Flusser, ibid., 149, and his preference for 'To the god who is in the district of the Danoi').

The Omphalos Myth

Jerusalem's unique place in the affections of biblical writers is reflected in various idealized references to its location and physical proportions. Two texts in Ezekiel (5:5; 38:12) have attracted special attention because of the possibility that they attest to the existence of a Hebrew equivalent of the classical Greek 'omphalos mythology'. According to this view, Jerusalem, as a specially sacred site, was regarded as standing at the centre (or 'navel') of Israel, or even of the whole earth. For some scholars these two texts form the core of a larger body of evidence that omphalos mythology plays a significant, or even central,[11] role in the Old Testament. The first reference lacks specific omphalos terminology, nevertheless God declares in Ezekiel 5:5 that he has set Jerusalem 'in the midst of the nations, with countries all around her'. Ezekiel 38:12, in the estimation of many scholars, is a full subscriber to omphalos mythology. There the intentions of Gog and his allies are disclosed: 'to plunder and loot and turn your hand against the resettled ruins and the people gathered from the nations, who have acquired livestock and goods and live at the *ṭabbûr* of the land (or "earth")'. In this latter case, Judges 9:37, referring to people coming down 'from the *ṭabbûr* of the land', is invariably drawn into the discussion.

Despite the strong advocacy that the theory has enjoyed, the case for omphalos mythology in Ezekiel, or anywhere else in the Old Testament, has not been demonstrated. In Ezekiel 5:5 the point is that God has made Jerusalem the centre of attention because of his own interest in her. That interest has its negative side, as the passage goes on to indicate. The prophet has already been enacting a symbolic siege of the city (see 4:1; 5:2), and in that respect 'the nations' are all about Jerusalem, and punishment will be 'in the sight of the nations' (5:8; cf. Amos 3:9–11, referring to Samaria).[12]

Strictly speaking, Gog's intention in Ezekiel 38:12 may not relate specifically to Jerusalem; he will come against 'the people gathered from the nations ... living at (or "on") the *ṭabbûr* of the land (or "earth")'. There are several other geographical terms in the chapter – 'mountains of Israel' (v. 8; cf. vv. 20, 21), 'land of unwalled villages' (v. 11), 'land of Israel' (v. 18) – that suggest that it is not just the capital city that is the focus of Gog's attack. In that case, it is not

---

[11] So S. Terrien, 'The Omphalos Myth and Hebrew Religion', *VT* 20 (1970), 315–38(317, 338).

[12] There is also a question about the force of the term *btwk*, translated above as 'in the midst of', since it can be shown to mean much the same as the simple preposition *b* ('in') in many passages. Perhaps the fuller sense is justified here by the context.

so obvious that the text is referring to Jerusalem as the centre or 'navel' of Israel. Much less can we be sure that Jerusalem is being located 'at the very centre of the world' (*REB*), since the Hebrew *'ereṣ* is at least as likely to denote the land of Israel as the earth in general.

There is also some doubt about the meaning of *ṭabbûr* in the biblical period. In post-biblical Hebrew the forms *ṭibbûr*[13] and *ṭabbûr* do indeed have the meaning 'navel', but we cannot assume this for the biblical occurrences of *ṭabbûr*.[14] At the same time, Biblical Hebrew has the word *šōr* with this meaning (cf. Ezek. 16:4). Furthermore, even if *ṭabbûr* meant 'navel' in classical Hebrew, there remains a question as to what it meant when used in a geographical sense, as in Judges 9 and Ezekiel 38. In Judges 9:37 Abimelech and his men are said to be 'coming down from the *ṭabbûr* of the land', which suggests that the expression is parallel to 'coming down from the tops of the mountains' in the preceding verse. And as we have seen, mountains are also important in Ezekiel 38 (see vv. 8, 20, 21). Centrality, then, may not necessarily be the dominant idea in the expression '*ṭabbûr* of the land', even if the biblical *ṭabbûr* were to mean 'navel'.

Link-Cities in Mesopotamia

The omphalos concept has what at first appears to be an ancient near eastern counterpart, and the two have sometimes been conflated as scholars have gone in pursuit of a widespread omphalos mythology in the ancient world. From the outset, however, we can note that the near eastern phenomenon is much older and is conceptually quite distinct. In Akkadian the key term is *markasu*, meaning 'rope', and then 'bond' or 'link', and it is used to express the idea of a specially important city or sanctuary being a link-point between the earth and the worlds below and above, as if connected to these latter by cosmic ropes.[15] The concept was known already in Sumer, hence the name Dur-an-ki ('Bond of heaven and earth') for its chief temple city Nippur. Babylon is similarly described as the *markasu*

---

[13] With this punctuation compare the reading *ṭybwr* from the Cairo Genizah fragment of Judges 9:37 cited in *BHS*.

[14] Although the LXX translates by 'omphalos', the Targum noticeably has *tqph* ('strength, fortress'), a translation that can scarcely have been made in ignorance of the meaning 'navel' but which may well have been made in rejection of it (cf. Peshitta 'beauty').

[15] Cf. R.J. Clifford, *The Cosmic Mountain in Canaan and the Old Testament* (Harvard Semitic Monographs, 4; Cambridge, MA: Harvard University Press, 1972), 15–16, 74.

kibrāti, 'link-point of the world', and the city of Asshur as _ša Aššur bēlšu ana kib-ra-a-te issuqaššu marka[ssu]_, '(the city) which Assur its lord has chosen to be the link-point of the whole world'.[16] Despite _CAD_'s inclusion of 'centre' as well as 'bond' in explanation of _markasu_, the idea that we are discussing is not that of a central location on a horizontal plane, but of link-points between the different levels of the universe. Centrality did not hold the same significance in Mesopotamia as it later did in classical and Jewish thinking. Even the Babylonian _mappa mundi_ from the early first millennium BC does not represent Babylon as being at the centre of the earth: Babylon is situated somewhat above the mid-point of the circular earth depicted on the tablet.[17] None of this relates, therefore, to omphalos mythology in the true sense. The ordinary Akkadian word for 'navel' (_abunnatu_) is used metaphorically of a geographical area and signifies the middle, or heart, of a country or, in another case, the centre, or middle, of an army.[18] These occurrences are, however, too few, and possibly also too indistinct, to be bracketed with omphalos-type references coming from further west and from a later period.

If we were to look for a biblical parallel to the link-city concept, Bethel, where the patriarch Jacob saw the 'ladder', or staircase, in his dream, is the obvious candidate.[19] The 'ladder' that Jacob sees in his dream extends from earth to heaven, and angels ascend and

---

[16] _The Assyrian Dictionary_, 8 (K) (Chicago: Oriental Institute, 1971), 332 (b 1).

[17] _pace_ Clifford, _The Cosmic Mountain_, 21. See O. Keel, _The Symbolism of the Biblical World: Ancient Near Eastern Iconography and the Book of Psalms_ (tr. T.J. Hallett; New York: Seabury Press, 1978), 21; J.M. Scott, _Geography in Early Judaism and Christianity: The Book of Jubilees_ (SNTSMS 113: Cambridge: Cambridge University Press, 2002), 10.

[18] M. Weinfeld also claims cosmological significance for _abunnatu_: 'The fact that Sumerian _dur_, which appears in a cosmological context, was rendered in Akkadian _abunnatu_ indicates that _abunnatu_ also had some cosmological significance' ('Zion and Jerusalem as Religious and Political Capital: Ideology and Utopia', in R.E. Friedman [ed.], _The Poet and the Historian: Essays in Literary and Historical Biblical Criticism_ [Harvard Semitic Studies, 26; Chico: Scholars Press, 1983], 106n. 53); cf. idem, 'The Roots of the Messianic Idea', in R.M. Whiting (ed.), _Mythology and Mythologies_ (Melammu Symposia, 2; Helsinki: The Neo-Assyrian Text Corpus Project, 2001), 279–87(285n. 31). See _The Assyrian Dictionary_, 1 (A/I) (Chicago: Oriental Institute, 1964), 89–90 (2).

[19] As already noted by D.J.A. Clines, 'Sacred Place, Holy Places and Suchlike', in _On the Way to the Postmodern: Old Testament Essays, 1967–1998. Volume II_ (SJSOT 293; Sheffield: Sheffield Academic Press, 1998), 543.

descend upon it as they commute between these two spheres. The importance of Bethel in the monarchical period as a cultic centre would, in Mesopotamian eyes, have qualified it for link-city status.

Omphalos in Post-biblical Texts

If there are strong doubts about the presence of omphalos mythology in the Old Testament, post-biblical Jewish writings amply compensate by incorporating it into their 'Zion theology', whether in outright contradiction of rival claims to omphalos status or simply in exposition of the importance of Jerusalem within the world order.[20] According to the *Letter of Aristeas* (83), Jerusalem was situated at the centre of Judea,[21] while 1 Enoch 26:1–2 locates the city in the middle of the earth.[22] Specific omphalos language comes in Jubilees 8:19, where Mount Zion is described as 'the centre of the navel of the earth',[23] and in Josephus' *War* 3:51–52, where it is noted that Jerusalem was sometimes called 'the omphalos' of the country (i.e. Judea).[24] So too, in the Babylonian Talmud, the Sanhedrin are said to have met at the navel of the world, i.e. Jerusalem.[25] In the post-biblical period, however, the

[20] Cf. P.S. Alexander, 'Jerusalem as the *Omphalos* of the World: On the History of a Geographical Concept', in L.I. Levine (ed.), *Jerusalem: Its Sanctity and Centrality to Judaism, Christianity, and Islam* (New York: Continuum, 1999), 104–19.

[21] Text in A. Pelletier (ed.), *Lettre d'Aristée à Philocrate* (Sources Chrétiennes, 89; Paris: Éditions du Cerf, 1962), 142–43. Cf. M. Tilly, 'Geographie und Weltordnung im Aristeasbrief', *JSJ* 28 (1997), 131–53(134). Tilly notes that there are points of correspondence between *Aristeas* 83–120 and Ezekiel 40–48, but does not regard direct dependence upon Ezekiel as likely (138–45).

[22] Cf. Philo, *Legatio* 294.

[23] 'He (sc. Noah) knew that the Garden of Eden is the holy of holies and is the residence of the Lord, that Mount Sinai is in the middle of the desert, and that Mount Zion is in the middle of the navel of the earth.' P.S. Alexander nominates Jubilees 8:19 as the earliest text that genuinely regards Jerusalem as the omphalos of the earth ('Jerusalem as the *Omphalos* of the World', 104–19[104–108]).

[24] The Josephan term may have influenced Isidore of Seville (c. 560–636) in his description of Jerusalem as the 'navel of the whole region': 'In medio autem Iudaeae civitas Hierosolyma est, quasi umbilicus regionis totius' (*Etymologiarum* 14:3:21); cf. Scott, *Geography in Early Judaism and Christianity*, 164.

[25] b. San. 37a (on Song 7:3). Cf. also A. Jellinek, *Bet-ha-Midrasch*, V (Vienna: Winter, 1873), 63, where God is said to have created the world like an embryo which begins its life at the navel. So the creation of the world began at its navel, Jerusalem.

influence of the Greek classical tradition may be assumed, with the Septuagint already translating both biblical occurrences of *ṭabbûr* by *omphalos* and thus assisting the development of Jewish omphalos mythology. Cohn argues that omphalos ideology replaced the Old Testament 'holy mountain' concept, reflecting the new theo-political reality of the Jewish diaspora, for whom a centre meant more than a summit.[26] This may be valid to some extent: omphalos ideology is certainly a new factor in the post-biblical era. Nevertheless, references to Zion as the highest of the mountains do continue into the rabbinic period,[27] and it was a feature of the biblical presentation of Mount Zion that it included a distinctly futuristic and global significance (cf. Isa. 2:1–4; Mic. 4:1–5).

Even if there is no omphalos mythology in the Old Testament, the unique place given Jerusalem in biblical thought does result in special claims being made on its behalf. The literal truth about the city is expressed in one of the 'Psalms of Ascents': 'Jerusalem – hills surround her' (Ps. 125:2); pilgrim travellers to the temple could not have failed to notice. In Psalm 125 the psalmist draws a comparison between a secure Jerusalem and the people whose hopes it embodies: 'As the mountains surround Jerusalem, so the Lord surrounds his people, both now and for evermore' (v. 2, *NIV*). These texts thus make a virtue of the fact that Jerusalem did not physically dominate its immediate surroundings. However, there are other texts in the Psalms and in the prophets that hyperbolize on the physical features of the city, the former directed to the then city and the latter envisaging its future greatness. This aspect of Jerusalem-Zion is addressed in following chapters.

---

[26] R.L. Cohn, *The Shape of Sacred Space: Four Biblical Studies* (American Academy of Religion Studies in Religion, 23; Chico: Scholars Press, 1981), 70–74 (cf. 55, 58); cf. Clifford, *The Cosmic Mountain*, 182.
[27] Cf. b. Kidd. 69a–b ('This teaches that the temple is higher than all the land of Israel and the land of Israel is higher than all the countries' [69a, with reference to Deut. 17:18]).

Chapter Four

How Did Psalm 48 Happen?

Earlier chapters have noted certain restrictions of language observed, for whatever reasons, by Old Testament writers where Jerusalem/Zion is concerned. We now move on to a psalm whose happy hyperbolizing about the 'city of God' sheds such restrictions, celebrating an idealized version of the city in the light of a great deliverance from enemy attack.

Psalm 48 belongs to the Korahite collection of psalms. It celebrates Zion, but more particularly the God of Zion, as its first ('Great is the Lord') and last ('This God is our God forever') verses indicate. Zion itself is viewed as a high mountain, 'beautiful for elevation' (v. 3[2]), though the language is modest as compared with the end-time elevation envisaged in some texts (cf. Isa. 2:2; Mic. 4:1; Zech. 14:10).[1] Moreover, some experience of God at his holy city has made the psalmist a believer in the invincibility of fortress Zion (cf. v. 9[8]). The nature of that experience commands no consensus among interpreters. Some, and especially earlier writers, assume a memorable deliverance from military attack, such as is represented in the biblical accounts of the Assyrian withdrawal from Jerusalem in 701 BC (cf. 2 Kgs. 19:35–36; Isa. 37:36–37).[2] Others think that a cultic re-enactment in line with the theme of God's triumph over his enemies was sufficient to inspire such thoughts in the psalmist. In

---

[1] Cf. also the 'very high mountain' seen by Ezekiel, on the south side of which 'was a structure like a city' (i.e. Jerusalem) (Ezek. 40:2). Some writers see a reference to the Jerusalem temple mount in the 'high and lofty mountain' of Isaiah 57:7 (cf. P.D. Hanson, *The Dawn of Apocalyptic: The Historical and Sociological Roots of Jewish Apocalyptic Eschatology* [Philadelphia: Fortress Press, 1975], 199–200). Neither the LXX nor the Peshitta is up to translating MT *yph nwp*, rendering by 'well planted' and 'praiseworthy' respectively.

[2] R.L. Cohn, 'The Mountains and Mount Zion', *Judaism* 26 (1977), 97–115(110), thinks that the opening verses of Psalm 48 celebrate Yahweh's defeat of the Canaanite god Baal on the historical plane, when David achieved the military successes attributed to him in 2 Samuel.

this latter case, it is allowed that an actual historical event may lie somewhere in the background, but it is still cultic enactment that is held to account for the language of the psalm.

This air of celebration contrasts profoundly with the atmosphere in Psalm 44, another member of the Korahite series. In Psalm 44, after a confident-sounding introduction (vv. 1–9[8]), the psalmist languishes in scarce-relieved gloom, with only the last word of the psalm (*ḥesed*, 'steadfast loyalty') offering any glimmer of light. The psalmist begins, 'We have heard with our ears, O God, our fathers have told us, what deeds you performed in their days, in the days of old', and he shows in what follows that he has the conquest-of-Canaan tradition in mind (vv. 3–4[2–3]). His complaint is that, for himself and his contemporaries, 'salvation-history' is second- and third-hand. We are reminded of Gideon in Judges 6:13: 'If the Lord is with us, why has all this happened to us? Where are all his wonders that our fathers told us about, when they said, "Did not the Lord bring us up out of Egypt?"' Psalm 78:3 similarly refers to 'things that we have heard and known, that our fathers told us'. In response to this kind of complaint about a defunct 'salvation-history' Psalm 48 makes its triumphant riposte: 'As we have heard, so have we seen.' 'Salvation-history' has happened again.

The Danite Hypothesis

Or so the more traditional kind of interpretation would have it. The difficulty with this is, however, that there does not appear to be anything in the historical tradition of the Old Testament that matches the terms of Psalm 48. So the option of a 'cultic event' begins to commend itself.[3] After all, it is when the attacking kings *see* Zion that they take fright (v. 6[5]); there is no mention of an encounter or of their defeat in battle. However, if it needed only a good service in the temple to cheer up saddened hearts, why the misery of the like of Psalm 44? When Psalm 44 declares that the psalmist and his contemporaries had been told of God's mighty acts by their 'fathers', this can scarcely refer to a declaration of the national *Heilsgeschichte* in the temple immediately prior to the recital of the psalm.[4]

Now, since what we are talking about could be portrayed as one of several mood swings within a closely linked series of (Korahite)

---

[3] Cf. Psalms 63:3[2]; 73:17, both of which speak of 'seeing' in the sanctuary.

[4] *pace* A. Weiser, *Die Psalmen. Erster Teil: Psalm 1–60* (4th edn; ATD 14; Göttingen: Vandenhoeck and Ruprecht, 1955), 239–40.

psalms, either it is a case of the external circumstances having altered, or we need a more sophisticated version of the temple service theory to account for the language of these psalms and for the relationships that exist among them. Such has, in fact, been outlined by J.P. Peters[5] and, more recently and at much greater length, by M.D. Goulder,[6] and what they offer – a festival liturgy – is certainly a plausible way to explain the mood swings within these psalms. In his 1922 study Peters had argued that the Korahite psalms originated as the liturgy for an eight-day celebration of the festival of Tabernacles in the northern sanctuary town of Dan. This liturgy had been introduced into the southern cultus after the fall of the northern kingdom in 722 BC. Goulder developed essentially the same thesis, independently of Peters, arguing the further point that there are in the Korahite series two parallel sets of psalms, the one having replaced the other as the Tabernacles liturgy, following a down-turn in the fortunes of the northern kingdom.

Geography of the 'Sacred Geography' sort has an important contribution to make to the interpretation of Psalm 48. It was geographical factors that largely accounted for Peters' original Danite hypothesis, since Zion is not known for either its elevation or its northernness, or for its river (cf. Ps. 46:5[4]), whereas the northern cult-centre of Dan much more obviously meets these specifications. Goulder notes that Mount Hermon, where Dan is located, 'outsoars the highest other mountain in Israel by three times, and the expression (sc. 'fair in height', v. 2) could have been made for it'.[7] However, given that there are other texts that hyperbolize on the physical features of Zion,[8] Psalm 48's description of it as 'fair in height', or 'beautiful for elevation', need cause no difficulty.[9] There is a still more striking case of *Babylon* being hyperbolized in Jeremiah 51:25 as a 'destroying mountain', which in no way could pass

[5] *The Psalms as Liturgies* (London: Hodder & Stoughton, 1922), 290–91.

[6] *The Psalms of the Sons of Korah* (SJSOT 20: Sheffield: JSOT Press, 1982).

[7] *The Psalms of the Sons of Korah*, 162. K. Seybold, 'Jerusalem in the View of the Psalms', in M. Poorthuis and Ch. Safrai (eds.), *The Centrality of Jerusalem: Historical Perspectives* (Kampen: Kok Pharos, 1996), 7–14(7), also holds to the northern origin of the Korahite psalms. M. Buss, 'The Psalms of Asaph and Korah', *JBL* 82 (1963), 382–92(387–88), locates their origin in Judah.

[8] See ch. 3.

[9] Indeed, A.P. Stanley was impressed by Jerusalem's natural location 'on the edge of one of the highest table-lands in the country' (*Sinai and Palestine in Connection with their History* [23rd edn; London: John Murray, 1918], 136).

for a literal description of the southern Mesopotamian environs of Babylon. The idea of Babylon as a mountain is sufficiently inappropriate as to suggest to a few scholars that the author knew nothing about the city and assumed that it was located on a hill, as Palestinian cities commonly were.[10] However, more often Babylon as 'mountain' has been taken to symbolize the city's military and political domination of the near east, or as containing an allusion to the heights of Zaphon, which in Isaiah 14:13 are represented as the ambitious goal of the king of Babylon.[11] Under the rubric of 'Sacred Geography', therefore, the description of Babylon as a mountain is by no means inappropriate,[12] and the same applies to Zion in Psalm 48.

Nor should the association of Zion with Zaphon/'the North' surprise us (v. 3[2]). For if it is the recesses (or heights) of Zaphon, and not just the cardinal point, that is in view, then the psalm is comparing Zion with the north Canaanite mountain associated with the god Baal.[13] Such a conflating of Zion and Zaphon may even find a parallel in the linking of the mountain of divine assembly and Mount Zaphon in Isaiah 14:13, where the 'Lucifer' figure says, 'I will sit on the mount of assembly, on the heights of Zaphon'.[14] In Psalm 48, then, the psalmist appears to be declaring that 'Zion is our Zaphon', or, in classical Greek terms, that 'Zion is our Mount Olympus'.

We may also recognize with Michael Barré an 'international' dimension to Psalm 48, in that Zion is described as 'the joy of the whole earth'[15] and 'the city of the Great King' (v. 3[2]).[16] This latter

---

[10] See W. McKane, *Jeremiah*, II (ICC; Edinburgh: T & T Clark, 1996), 1315.

[11] Cf. P. Volz, *Der Prophet Jeremia* (KAT 10; Leipzig: A. Deichertsche Verlagsbuchhandlung, 1922), 431.

[12] Cf. M. Kessler, *Battle of the Gods: The God of Israel Versus Marduk of Babylon. A Literary/Theological Interpretation of Jeremiah 50–51* (Studia Semitica Neerlandica; Assen: Royal Van Gorcum, 2003), 119–20.

[13] See Anat and Baal 4:19; 5:117, etc. A very different view was expressed by J.J.S. Perowne, *The Book of Psalms* (6th edn; London: George Bell, 1888), 190: 'But for a Jew to speak of Zion, the holy mountain, as if it were no more than some mountain of heathen fable, would have been nothing short of profanity.'

[14] Cf. J. Day, *God's Conflict with the Dragon and the Sea: Echoes of a Canaanite Myth in the Old Testament* (University of Cambridge Oriental Publications, 35; Cambridge: Cambridge University Press, 1982), 117n. 114, 132–33.

[15] Cf. Lam. 2:15 where, in the context of destruction and exile, the epithet 'joy of the whole earth' adds to the reproach of Jerusalem trodden down.

[16] M.L. Barré, 'The Seven Epithets of Zion in Ps 48,2–3', *Biblica* 69 (1988), 557–63(559–60).

expression may be based on near eastern imperial titles of the *šarru rabû* type, as seems clearly to be the case in Malachi 1:14 where God declares that he is the 'great king' and, by implication, more deserving of honour than the regional Persian governor whom he mentions in the same section ('Try offering [your blemished sacrifices] to your governor!', v. 8 [cf. *NIV*]). This apart, in the Korahite Psalm 47 God is described as the 'great king over all the earth' (v. 3[2]; cf. Ps. 95:3). A comparison with, or annexation of, Canaanite Zaphon 'theology' would fit very well with an international emphasis in Psalm 48. Barré goes on to suggest that *nwp* in the phrase *yph nwp* ('beautiful for elevation') is actually a reference to Memphis ('Noph' or 'Moph' in Biblical Hebrew) in Egypt – 'Beautiful Memphis' – and so provides a southern correlate to northern Zaphon.[17] This is unconvincing, but we need not be persuaded by it in order to appreciate the international scope of these verses – an international dimension that has been noted by others who have not felt obliged to bring Memphis into the picture.

Hyperbole and History

The hyperbole of 'Sacred Geography' in Psalm 48 sits well with yet other hyperbolical elements in the psalm. This holds especially for vv. 5–8(4–7) and the question whether there is an historical experience of deliverance behind these verses, or simply a cultic celebration that itself may have drawn upon mythological motifs from the old *Völkerkampf* tradition. In verses 5–6(4–5) kings are said to have banded together,[18] but then to have witnessed something that sent them into headlong flight. The common objection to the historical experience interpretation is, as we have noted, that there is nothing recorded in the Old Testament that could have generated a reference of this sort: there is no coalition of kings against Jerusalem such as the psalm envisages.[19] The problem with this approach is that it is too prosaic, making no allowance for the kind of poetic hyperbole that we have already found in verse 3(2). In order to find the missing plurality ('kings') somewhere in the tradition, it is occasionally noted that the king of Assyria boasts in Isaiah 10:8, 'Are not my commanders all kings?', which is apparently intended to

---

[17] 'The Seven Epithets', 561–62. So also N. Wyatt, 'Le centre du monde dans les littératures d'Ougarit et d'Israël', *JNSL* 21 (1995), 123–42(126–27) ('aussi belle que Memphis' [126]).

[18] The LXX A text makes them 'the kings of the earth', presumably under the influence of Psalm 2:2.

[19] Cf. Weiser, *Die Psalmen*, 257.

exalt the Assyrian generals at the expense of the kings of the Levantine states. We might even more usefully consider the battle between the armies of the king of Hazor and the Israelites as described in Judges 4 and in the hymnic celebration of the battle in the next chapter. The prose account is of an Israelite victory over a general who is at the head of the army of a Canaanite city-state ruler, but the hymn that accompanies the narrative claims that 'the *kings* of Canaan' came and fought at Taanach by the waters of Megiddo, 'but they carried off no spoils of silver' (Judg. 5:19).

Nothing in Judges 4 warrants the assumption by some commentators that Jabin summoned a coalition of nearby rulers against the Israelites – as is described for an earlier member of his dynasty in Joshua 11 – for the battle account knows only the apparently absentee Canaanite king of Hazor and Sisera, the general who actually engaged with the Israelite tribesmen. In the reference to Canaanite 'kings' in Judges 5:19, therefore, poetic hyperbole is at work, as overwhelmingly in the next verse, which says that 'the stars fought from heaven' against Sisera.[20]

The kings of Psalm 48 'saw', but what they saw is not expressed. If the cultic re-enactment interpretation is pursued, the psalm is saying that the worshippers 'saw' (v. 9[8]), and that what they saw included a representation of the assembled kings 'seeing' whatever it was that threw them into panic (v. 6[5]). This begins to take on the character of a hall of mirrors, whereas perhaps it is simply the awesome sight of literal Zion that unnerves the kings, and the worshippers are claiming to have witnessed their discomfiture.[21] This could, of course, relate to an historical experience that has been filtered through the lens of Israelite faith and hyperbole. The use of the adverb 'there' (v. 7[6]) may imply something more definite than mere cultic re-enactment, as Goulder notes,[22] and we might also compare Psalm 76:3–4(2–3) in this respect:

---

[20] Psalm 68 has similar references to discomfited kings (vv. 13[12], 15[14]), and although the description of the psalm, or of sections within it, cannot be done with much confidence, verses 12–15(11–14) could be read as recapitulation of the conquest tradition of the Judges period. Earlier commentators especially were happy to link these verses with the celebratory song of Judges 5, in which case the use of the plural in 'kings' provided a direct parallel to Judges 5:19. However, even if Psalm 68:12–15(11–14) is referring to the 'conquest period', more appears to be in view than the particular episode of Judges 4–5.

[21] Cf. *NIV*'s insertion of 'her' ('they saw [her]') (v. 6[5]) in reference to Jerusalem-Zion.

[22] *The Psalms of the Sons of Korah*, 165. The Peshitta lacks the word, but it is represented in the LXX.

(3[2]) His tent is in Salem,
   his dwelling in Zion.
(4[3]) There[23] he broke the flashing arrows,
   the shields and the swords, the weapons of war.

Of course, it would be possible to insist that Zion is, in both cases, the location of a mythological victory celebrated in the temple worship as the sign and symbol of Zion's inviolability.

Psalm 48:8(7) introduces another problem with its mention of the destruction of ships of Tarshish by the agency of the east wind. What, we may ask, has enemy shipwreck got to do with the doctrine of the invincibility of Zion? As is well-known, Morgenstern saw in this a reference to the destruction of a good part of Xerxes' Persian fleet just prior to the battle of Artemisium in 480 BC when, according to Herodotus, the east wind ('the Hellespontian') wrought havoc.[24] 'Ships of Tarshish' were, according to 2 Chronicles 20:37, ships that went to Tarshish. They were relatively large and imposing, and were symbols of power and pretension. In Isaiah 2:16 God 'has a day against' (cf. v. 12) the ships of Tarshish, as well as against other symbols of human self-esteem mentioned in the surrounding verses. 2 Chronicles 20:35–37 notes that when Jehoshaphat of Judah made an alliance with Ahaziah of Israel they had ships of Tarshish constructed at Ezion Geber. The ships, however, were 'broken' (*šbr* as in Ps. 48:8[7]), in accordance with a word of prophecy from Eliezer of Mareshah.[25]

Translational uncertainties also affect the interpretation of Psalm 48:8(7). First, it is possible to treat the reference to the east wind and the ships of Tarshish as simile rather than direct predication, and, secondly, the psalmist switches from his prior use of suffixed tenses to the prefixed tense in *tšbr* ('break', 'smash'). A look at representative versions ancient and modern will indicate the way in which interpretation is affected by these two factors:

---

[23] *NEB* takes *šmh* as a verb-form and connects with the preceding clause in verse 2 ('in Zion his battle-quarters *are set up*'), noting that the MT has 'thither' at the beginning of verse 3. This, however, fails to recognize that *šmh* is sometimes used without directional significance and means simply 'there'.

[24] J. Morgenstern, 'Psalm 48', *HUCA* 16 (1941), 1–95(6–10). See Herodotus, *Histories*, 7:188, 190–91. Morgenstern recognizes a separate psalm fragment ('Psalm 48B') in the MT of verses 5–8.

[25] Here in Psalm 48 the east wind is the agent of destruction (cf. Exod. 10:13; 14:21; Isaiah 27:8; Jer. 18:17; Ezek. 17:10; 27:26 [of ship Tyre]; Ps. 78:26; Job 27:21).

LXX	With a strong wind you will smash the ships of Tarshish
AV	Thou breakest the ships of Tarshish with an east wind
RV	With the east wind thou breakest the ships of Tarshish
NIV	You destroyed them like ships of Tarshish shattered by an east wind
NRSV	as when an east wind shatters the ships of Tarshish[26]
REB	like the ships of Tarshish when an east wind wrecks them

What this sampling shows is that the psalmist may not be referring to a past event in this verse, whether because of the tense used or because of his possible use of simile, or for both reasons together. The LXX translates *tšbr* with a future,[27] the *AV* and *RV* use the present and so are not committed to a specific past event,[28] while *NIV*, *NRSV* and *REB* treat the mention of the ships as simile, so providing a parallel to verse 7b(6b) where the writhing kings are compared to a woman in labour.[29] This recognition of a simile more or less removes the possibility of a reference to an historical event involving actual ships of Tarshish. *REB* and *NRSV* noticeably also make 'wind' the subject of 'break', so eliminating the second-person reference[30] and therewith any explicit reference to divine action in the verse. *NIV* differs from the rest in its translation of the prefixed tense by the past, and this is perfectly defensible in poetry, though certainly not the only possibility. The same version's supplying of 'them' (i.e. the kings) as the object of 'destroyed' is not impossible, but since the *NIV* rendering of the verse is not the only possible one, it cannot be used to support the view that the ships of Tarshish function only as a simile. At the same time, as we have noted, the case for seeing verse 8(7) as depicting an overthrow of ships of Tarshish,

---

[26] Cf. H.-J. Kraus, *Psalmen*, I (BKAT 15/1; Neukirchen: Neukirchener Verlag, 1960), 355: 'wie der Ostwind zerschmettert die Tarsisschiffe'.

[27] This is probably also the intention behind the Peshitta version's *nttbrn*.

[28] Goulder, *The Psalms of the Sons of Korah*, 165, suggests that 'the change of tense to the imperfect in verse 7 signifies that such shipwrecks occur frequently'.

[29] Perhaps most elegantly expressed in *REB*: 'they toss in pain like a woman in labour, like the ships of Tarshish when an east wind wrecks them'.

[30] Otherwise there is no second-person address until verse 10(9). For the east wind as subject of verbs of destruction see Ezekiel 27:26; Job 27:21.

whether historically or even in some cultic portrayal, is far from clear-cut.[31] Doubt is therefore cast on Gerstenberger's fairly confident surmise that the mention of ships points to the origins of the 'myth' in verses 5–8(4–7) in the coastal regions of northern Syria.[32]

The translation of *dimmînû* in verse 10(9) is also relevant to this discussion, especially since *NEB*, following A.R. Johnson,[33] offers 'O God, we re-enact the story of thy true love within thy temple.' However, the fact that *dimmînû* has the abstract *ḥesed* ('steadfast love') as its object should put limits on speculation.[34] *REB* restores sobriety with, 'God, within your temple we meditate on your steadfast love.' Although there is no exact parallel to the occurrence in Psalm 48:10(9), the verb *dāmāh* occurs with the meaning 'think, reckon' in Esther 4:13, and so the 'problem' of *dimmînû* can be overstated. The development of thought in Psalm 48 is, then, much as in Psalm 77:12–13(11–12): 'I will call to mind the deeds of the Lord ... I will meditate (*hgh*) on all your work' (cf. Pss. 63:[7]6; 143:5; 145:5).

Finally, verse 13(14) raises a serious point in relation to the historical event versus cultic experience discussion. Are we really to

---

[31] Day, *God's Conflict with the Dragon*, 128–29, rejects the simile option, arguing that Isaiah 33:21 ('But there the majestic Lord will be for us a place of rivers and broad streams where no ship with oars can go or stately vessel pass') speaks of eschatological Zion as 'inviolable to attack by ship' (128), thus showing that ships can be brought into association with Zion mythologically, without the involvement of simile. However, what is described in the respective texts is sufficiently different to discourage any attempt to use the Isaiah reference as a clinching argument for the interpretation of Psalm 48:8(7). It is perhaps going too far to say that 'the ships are defeated within sight of the city' (Day, 127), since verse 9(8) ('as we have heard, so have we seen') could refer to the sequence of events in verses 5(4)–7(6), and the more so if verse 9(8) is taken as simile or is translated in the present tense (cf. *AV, RV*).

[32] E.S. Gerstenberger, *Psalms: Part 1, With an Introduction to Cultic Poetry* (The Formation of the Old Testament Literature, 14; Grand Rapids: Eerdmans, 1988), 201; cf., already, Day, *God's Conflict with the Dragon*, 127–28.

[33] A.R. Johnson, *The Cultic Prophet in Ancient Israel* (2nd edn; Cardiff: University of Wales Press, 1962), 42–43 ('O God, we have pictured Thy devotion/In the midst of Thy Temple' [43]).

[34] J.D. Levenson cites the noun *dᵉmût* ('likeness') in support of the meaning 'form a mental picture': 'The pilgrims of Psalm 48 affirm...that they have formed a mental picture of [God's] faithful care (v 10) through their inspection of his Temple' (*Sinai and Zion: An Entry into the Jewish Bible* [New Voices in Biblical Studies; Minneapolis: Winston Press, 1985], 149–50[150]).

regard this recounting as a reporting back to under-aged children on what they have missed at Jerusalem – principally the service and the architecture?[35] If the verse is talking about the transmission of sacred tradition down the generations, as interpreters easily and naturally assume, then it is surely not just the special temple celebration or even the citadels that need reporting to future generations for whom these – by definition, in view of this psalm's position on Zion's invincibility – would be equally accessible. On the other hand, it would make sense to pass on traditions of historical events associated with the citadels and commemorated in temple services.

The question posed by Psalm 48 is not simply whether we have spontaneous hyperbolizing in the wake of historical experience or the historicizing of myth in order to encapsulate some historical moment. Rather, there is a more fundamental issue here: the danger of dissolving psalm references of an apparently historical character into cultic performances, when sometimes they may well be psalmists' responses to historical events as they perceived them. The point is that theophanic-type language may serve historical reportage, just as happens in Judges 5 where the language of theophany and the celebration of an historical event as perceived by the poet come together in the one composition. So, although I am not persuaded by Goulder's quite brilliant exposition of the possible Danite connections of Psalm 48, I do find his attempt to preserve an historical dimension for the psalm convincing.[36] The types of references upon which a cultic re-enactment explanation of Psalm 48:5–8(4–7) is sometimes based[37] belong in a different category and do not even sound as if they are meant to reflect historical events and circumstances.

Psalm 48, then, comes in answer to the familiar dilemma of the faithful: the absence of the signs of divine presence in the way that tradition has reported them from earlier generations. 'So have we seen' (v. 9[8]), far from simply commemorating a cultic experience summarized in the verses immediately preceding, is the psalmist's answer to that condition of merely having 'heard', but not having 'seen', so powerfully voiced in Psalm 44 ('But you have rejected and humbled us', v. 10[9]).

The report of the deliverance that has been experienced is to radiate from Zion both spatially and chronologically: to the towns

---

[35] So Weiser, *Die Psalmen*, 258; cf. Gerstenberger, *Psalms: Part 1*, 202: 'It is important, too, that the procession or its purpose and contents is to be reported to the descendants.'
[36] *The Psalms of the Sons of Korah*, 164–65.
[37] Cf. Gerstenberger, *Psalms: Part 1*, 201.

and villages ('daughters') of Judah (v. 12[11]) and on to the next generation (v. 14[13]). Yet, as we have already noted, the psalmist wishes to point beyond the city and its fortifications to the delivering God who is Zion's ultimate source of security (vv. 4[3], 15[14]). The psalm has commonly been dated to the pre-exilic period on the not unreasonable grounds that after the Babylonian destruction it would have been much more difficult for a Judean psalmist to extol the city's invincibility in the face of enemy attack. Gerstenberger, however, argues for a post-exilic origin because of what he takes to be 'a full-fledged Zion ideology that makes Jerusalem the absolute center of the world'.[38] We have already seen, nevertheless, that such an 'omphalos' view of Zion does not exist anywhere in the Old Testament,[39] whatever the period, and it is certainly not expressed in Psalm 48.

In conclusion: while the portrayal of God's triumph over chaos and evil in mythic terms is a feature of the Psalter, it is also the case that mythic language can be used in the portrayal of events within history. In Psalm 48 the language is as much hyperbolical as mythic, and the likelihood is that the psalm is the product of historical reminiscence as well as cultic celebration.

Our next chapter will show how a place and an event in history became hyperbolized in the way of Jerusalem/Zion – and yet far in excess of the Zion of Psalm 48 – in token of their unique importance for Christian faith.

---

[38] *Psalms: Part 1*, 202.
[39] See ch. 3.

Chapter Five

The Geography of Golgotha

Up to this point our attention has been focused on the Old Testament. This chapter marks a break in the discussion by turning to the central event narrated and expounded in the books of the New Testament. Apart from the intrinsic importance of the subject, and its appropriateness in a discussion of the interplay between geography and theology, we shall find that the major hyperbolizing themes that the Old Testament associates with Jerusalem/Zion are, in Christian hands, transferred to the place of Christ's crucifixion where, according to an ancient tradition of interpretation, salvation was achieved 'in the midst of the earth' (cf. Ps. 74:12). There have also been complicating issues relating to the identification and superintendence of the sites that have come to be associated with the Crucifixion, as the first part of the chapter indicates.

A certain amount of information on the location of Golgotha is provided by New Testament writers. First, the name itself is deserving of comment, for in three of the Gospel crucifixion narratives (Mt. 27:33; Mk 15:22; Jn 19:17) it is called 'The Place of a Skull', whereas in Luke 23:33 it is referred to as 'the place called Skull'. Since the singular number is consistently used – 'Skull' not 'Skulls' – there is force in the old argument that the name is not really compatible with the idea of a dumping-ground for corpses. Perhaps a skull-like rock configuration is implied, as is often enough suggested.

The indications are that Golgotha was situated outside the city walls of Jerusalem (Mt. 27:31–32; Jn 19:16–17), but yet not far from the city (Jn 19:20). This datum was known to the writer of Hebrews, for whom it was theologically significant that Christ 'suffered outside the gate in order to sanctify the people through his own blood' (13:12). Here the expression 'outside the gate' parallels 'outside the camp' in the preceding verse. This represents a natural and easy equating of the Israelite camp of the wilderness phase with the city of Jerusalem, as can also be illustrated from a Qumran text.[1]

---

[1] See E. Qimron and J. Strugnell (eds.), *Qumran Cave 4: V, Miqsat Ma'ase Ha-Torah* (DJD 10; Oxford: Clarendon, 1994), 48–51: 'And we think that

The Raising of Golgotha

Whatever the exact location of Golgotha, the hyperbole of 'Sacred Geography' appears to have affected its depiction in Christian piety and hymnology not least, for there is no basis in the New Testament writings for the familiar description of Golgotha as a 'hill' or 'mountain'. Indeed, it is noticeable that, when a New Testament writer mentions 'the holy mountain', he is referring to the 'Mount of Transfiguration' (2 Pet. 1:18). The use of the term in one connection would not, of course, prohibit its use in another, nevertheless it is a fact that hill-mountain language is not used for Golgotha anywhere in the New Testament. The most that can be said is that the place of crucifixion was visible from a distance (cf. Mk 15:40; Lk. 23:49). It is the Bordeaux Pilgrim who, in the fourth century, first refers to the elevation of Golgotha: *A sinistra autem parte est monticulus Golgotha, ubi Dominus crucifixus est* ('On the left side [as one goes out of the city] is the little hill of Golgotha where the Lord was crucified'). That the pilgrim is not the most scientifically astute observer and reporter of Palestinian topography need not worry us,[2] since it is simply the beginnings of a tradition that we are observing. Not many decades later, Jerome in his letter to Paulinus refers to the marble statue of Venus erected 'in Crucis rupe' ('on the rock of the Cross').[3]

Early in the fifth century Rufinus, in his translation into Latin of the *Ecclesiastical History* of Eusebius, also uses the word 'rupes' ('rock') of Golgotha. Rufinus translated the *History* early in the first decade of the fifth century, at the request of Chromatius, bishop in his hometown of Aquileia.[4] He took great liberties with Eusebius' Greek text, occasionally adding information from personal observation made during his stay in a number of major centres. Thus he is able to supplement Eusebius by including a reference to the Constantinian basilicas constructed in Rome in honour of St Peter and St Paul (*EH* 2:25). Since Rufinus spent as much as eighteen years (AD 379–397) in Jerusalem,[5] his comments on Jerusalem topography can be taken

---

[1] (*continued*) the sanctuary [is the tent of meeting and that J]erusale[m] is the "camp", and that "out[side] the camp" [is outside Jerusalem], that is, the encampment of their cities' (lines 29–30).

[2] For example, the transfiguration of Christ is associated with the Mount of Olives.

[3] *Epistola ad Paulinum* (PL 22, col. 581).

[4] See J.E.L. Oulton, 'Rufinus's Translation of the Church History of Eusebius', *JTS* 30 (1928–29), 150–74.

[5] So Oulton, 'Rufinus's Translation', 151.

with equal seriousness. He updates Eusebius' information about the burial-place of Queen Helena of Adiabene (*EH* 2:12), and when referring to Christ's death associates it with the 'Golgothana rupes' ('the rock of Golgotha').[6] Such are the beginnings of a long tradition of representing Golgotha as a hill or mountain.

Golgotha, Gobat and Gordon

Although serious reconfiguration of the general area in the first and second centuries is known to have occurred as a result of the Roman destructions of Jerusalem, it is very questionable whether 'hill' was ever appropriate in description of Golgotha. On the other hand, the rock formation in the area of the Church of the Holy Sepulchre may be sufficient to account for the Bordeaux Pilgrim's 'monticulus' and the 'rupes' of Jerome and Rufinus. Representations of Golgotha from two or three centuries later display the cross surmounting a rock, for example on an ampulla from the sixth or seventh century and on a marble plaque from the same period.[7]

The Golgotha-hill connection entered a new phase with General Charles Gordon's arrival in Jerusalem on 17 January 1883.[8] Gordon stayed in the Jerusalem area for several months, basing himself in the village of Ein Kerem/Ain Karim and remaining there until his move to Jaffa in July of 1883.[9] During this period he wrote voluminously to his friends about his experiences, sharing with them his ideas on a host of biblical topics. He was steeped in the language of the Authorized Version of the Bible and was a keen contributor to theories about biblical locations. Some of his thoughts were published in an article entitled 'Eden and Golgotha' that

---

[6] Text in E. Schwartz and Th. Mommsen (eds.), *Die Griechischen Christlichen Schriftsteller der Ersten Drei Jahrhunderte. Eusebius*, II.2 (Leipzig: J.C. Hinrichs, 1908), 815 (9:6:3).

[7] See M. Biddle, *The Tomb of Christ* (Stroud: Sutton Publishing, 1999), 23 (fig. 20), 24 (no. 7), 26 (fig. 24; no. 10).

[8] For discussion of Gordon's time in Palestine see Lord Elton, *General Gordon* (London: Collins, 1954), 312–23; J. Pollock, *Gordon: The Man Behind the Legend* (London: Constable, 1993), 252–59. For brief reference to Gordon and a fuller account of the context in which his advocacy of 'Gordon's Calvary' began, see N.A. Silberman, *Digging for God and Country: Exploration, Archeology, and the Secret Struggle for the Holy Land 1799–1917* (New York: Doubleday, 1982), 147–60(152–53).

[9] On 28 January he wrote, 'I am in my new house at Ain Karin (*sic*), three miles from Jerusalem'; see *Letters of General C.G. Gordon to his Sister M.A. Gordon* (London: Macmillan, 1888), 296.

appeared in the *Palestine Exploration Fund Quarterly Statement* 1885 (pp. 78–81). The article seems to represent two different despatches from his eastern travels,[10] the first being headed 'Position of Eden' (p. 78) and the second, simply, 'Golgotha' (pp. 79–81). In the former, Gordon finds the 'District of Eden' out in the Indian Ocean and appears confident about the botanical names of the Tree of Knowledge and the Tree of Life.

By 1883 there were already two main claimants for recognition as Golgotha – the site at the Church of the Holy Sepulchre and what Gordon calls 'Skull Hill' in his despatch of that year. Back in 1841 the American historical geographer Edward Robinson, in his *Biblical Researches in Palestine*, had poured a douche of cold water on the Church of the Holy Sepulchre as Christ's burial place,[11] and this helped clear the ground for the alternative that is enthusiastically canvassed by some Christians to this day. The claims of the hill above 'Jeremiah's Grotto', not far from Damascus Gate, appear to have been first advocated by Otto Thenius in 1842,[12] in an article in which he outlined the weaknesses of the traditional identification and wrote at some length about the new proposal. Others quickly followed, and even the rationalist Ernest Renan declared the identification 'allowable' in later editions of his *Vie de Jésus*, first published in

---

[10] Cf. p. 79: 'I last wrote to you giving the four rivers of Eden, one of which was the Gihon on which Jerusalem was.' This forms the subject-matter of p. 78 ('Position of Eden').

[11] *Biblical Researches in Palestine, Mount Sinai and Arabia Petraea: A Journal of Travels in the Year 1838*, I (3 vols.; London: John Murray, 1841). Some of Robinson's reactions to what he witnessed at the Church of the Holy Sepulchre are noted in his diary for Easter Day, 15 April 1838, and bear repetition: 'I was struck with the splendour of their robes ... but I was not less struck with the vulgar and unmeaning visages that peered out from these costly vestments. The wearers looked more like ordinary ruffians than like ministers of the cross of Christ' (330); 'even the monks themselves do not pretend that the present sepulchre is any thing more than an imitation of the original' (331). Robinson then notes that he did not visit the place again.

[12] Not 1849 as sometimes claimed in references which usually do not give the source of the purported information. See 'De Golgotha et Sancto Sepulcro' (short title), *Zeitschrift für die historische Theologie* 12/4 (1842), 3–34(16–34). It is interesting to read the report of Edward Robinson on his visit to the area – specifically to Jeremiah's Grotto – on 18 April 1838: the grotto 'lies under a round isolated rocky hill, the south side of which has apparently been cut away to an irregular face, under which is the entrance to the grotto. In front is a small garden walled in ...' (*Biblical Researches*, 345).

1863.[13] Gordon appears to have known of the spot favoured by Thenius and others (see below), since he set out for 'Skull Hill' on the morning after his arrival in Jerusalem, and very quickly decided that this must be the place of the Crucifixion. As he wrote to his sister Augusta that same day (18 January), 'It is very nice to have it so plain and simple, instead of having a huge church built on it.'[14] It is easy to assume that Gordon was attracted by the physiognomical (that is, face-like) features of 'Gordon's Calvary' that so often impress the visitor to the site, whereas he makes nothing of this[15] in his communication to the Palestine Exploration Fund. He is even reported by Sir Charles Wilson as having dismissed the idea in a private letter. He was more influenced by the configuration of the hill as it was represented on the Ordnance Survey plan of Jerusalem for 1864–65.[16]

The argument by which Gordon defended his decision in *PEFQS* 1885 is remarkable, depending upon a form of typological interpretation of the Old Testament that, if unheard of now, was not so rare in his day. Because Leviticus 1:11 says that burnt offerings were to be slaughtered on the north side of the altar in the tabernacle or temple court, Gordon was convinced that this must have a bearing on the location of the Crucifixion: 'if a particular direction was given by God about where the types were to be slain, it is a sure deduction that the prototype would be slain in some position as to the Altar: this the Skull Hill fulfils'.[17] Here the words 'in some

---

[13] 'Il serait loisible aussi de penser au monticule qui domine la "Grotte de Jérémie"' (*Vie de Jésus* [14th edn; Paris: Michel Lévy, 1873], 429n. 2).

[14] *Letters*, 290. Gordon's willingness to recognize a more worthy site than the then infamous 'Holy Sepulchre' area as the place of Christ's crucifixion is paralleled in the comments of other non-Catholic visitors to Jerusalem. In his *Rambles in Bible Lands* (London: Charles H. Kelly, 1891), Richard Newton offers his own withering comments on what he witnessed: 'we felt our hearts sicken within us to think of the depth of human credulity on the one hand, and the utter shamelessness of the priests in ministering to that credulity on the other' (45); 'At the Easter festival in 1834, a fight took place in this church which resulted in the death of four hundred people. In the earlier ages of the Church, the enemies of the Gospel, as they saw the strength of the tie which bound the followers of Jesus together, were forced to exclaim, "See how these Christians love one another!"' (46). See also note 11 above.

[15] Cf. G. Dalman, *Sacred Sites and Ways: Studies in the Topography of the Gospels* (tr. P.P. Levertoff; London: SPCK, 1935), 348n. 5.

[16] Sir Charles W. Wilson, 'Golgotha and the Holy Sepulchre' [*concluded*], *PEFQS* 1904, 26–41(41); idem, *Golgotha and the Holy Sepulchre* (ed. C.M. Watson; London: Palestine Exploration Fund, 1906), 12.

[17] 'Eden and Golgotha', *PEFQS* 1885, 78–81(79).

position' are significant, for Gordon did not understand Leviticus
1:11 to say simply that the burnt offerings were to be killed on the
north side of the altar, which is how the reference is normally understood. Instead, he says, parenthetically, that the offerings were 'literally to be slain slantwise or askew on the north of the Altar'.[18] He
then appeals to Isaiah 65:2 ('all the day long have I stretched out my
arms to a rebellious people') and thereafter explains how the verse
relates to his previous statement.

> Draw a line from the centre of the Sakhra[19] to the centre of the Skull;
> draw a perpendicular to this line, at centre of skull; a cross on that line
> will embrace all the city and Mount of Olives, and be askew to the
> Altar.[20]

He had written along similar lines in his letter of 18 January to his
sister. Here he notes that the Temple and much else in Jerusalem
would have been visible from 'Skull Hill', and so '[Christ's]
stretched-out arms would, as it were, embrace it all the day: "all day
long have I stretched out my arms".'[21] The result is the typological
justification of 'Skull Hill', or 'Gordon's Calvary', on the northern
side of the city, as the place of the Crucifixion. Gordon then
observes that the 'Latin Holy Sepulchre' is 'west of the Altar' and
therefore not compatible with the typology. Psalm 48 even comes
into play, for Gordon deduces from the Gospels references to 'The
Place of a Skull' that other topographical features in the area make
up the shape of a human skeleton.[22] So the Septuagint translation of
yrkty ('recesses [of Zaphon]') in Psalm 48:3(2) by *pleura* ('sides')
relates to this figure, though the reasoning at this point is not untyp-
ically convoluted.

 If all this sounds too far-fetched, in one respect Gordon was certainly not out on his own. The typological argument from the place
of sacrifice on the north side of the altar of burnt offering in the
temple had advocates before and after 1883. Sir Charles Wilson, in

---

[18] On this Sir Charles Wilson comments: 'The interpretation of Lev. i, 11 is
erroneous. The words mean that the victim was to be slain north and not
north-north-west of the altar' ('Golgotha', 41n. 2).

[19] This is the rock formation housed in the so-called 'Dome of the Rock'
within the Old City in Jerusalem.

[20] 'Eden and Golgotha', *PEFQS* 1885, 79.

[21] See also Gordon's *Reflections in Palestine. 1883* (London: Macmillan,
1884), 3, where the Isaiah reference is quoted from Romans 10:21.

[22] '[I]f the skull is mentioned four times, one naturally looks for the body'
('Eden and Golgotha', *PEFQS* 1885, 79–80); cf. *Reflections*, 7–8. Pollock,
Gordon, 254, puts it quite elegantly: 'he worked out that the ridge running
south west from this hill to the Temple area, where the mosques now
stood, had the form of a human skeleton and he saw a mystic meaning'.

his article 'Jerusalem' in the second edition of Sir William Smith's *A Dictionary of the Bible* (1893), rejected 'Gordon's Calvary', and yet twice cited the typological argument from Leviticus 1:11 as a potentially significant factor in the correct identification of Golgotha.[23] He associates the view with Bishop Samuel Gobat who was Bishop of Jerusalem from 1846 to 1879.[24] Gobat firmly rejected the claim of the Church of the Holy Sepulchre to incorporate the site of the Crucifixion, and he was even willing to incur the wrath of Frederick William IV of Prussia on the matter. He had spent Holy Week in 1827 in close attendance at the traditional site and was nauseated by the superstitions and perversions of Christian teaching that were enacted then: 'That Holy Week was the most melancholy week of my life.'[25] At his audience with the king, Gobat recalled the experience and declared that it was a relief to know that the actual tomb of Christ lay somewhere else.[26] Thus, although one has not found direct evidence of Gobat's typological approach to the locating of Golgotha, Wilson's association of it with Gobat sounds altogether reasonable. It is not surprising, either, that Gobat is reported by a friend from his Jerusalem days as tending not to become involved in discussions with visitors about Jerusalem topography.[27]

The 'Third Wall'

'Gordon's Calvary', as it became known, has the attraction of being located outside the present Old City of Jerusalem, and so conveys an impression of the original that is denied the Church of the Holy Sepulchre, despite its stronger claims to authenticity.[28] However, it

---

[23] Art. 'Jerusalem' in *A Dictionary of the Bible* (ed. W. Smith and J.M. Fuller; 2nd edn; London: John Murray, 1893), 1655–66. Cf. also Wilson, 'Golgotha', 38.

[24] See also Wilson, *Golgotha*, 34n. 6, 119.

[25] *Samuel Gobat, Bishop of Jerusalem: His Life and Work. A Biographical Sketch, Drawn Chiefly from His Own Journals* (London: James Nisbet, 1884), 78–79.

[26] 'I once spent the entire Holy Week, even several nights of it, in the church of the so-called Holy Sepulchre, and after seeing the abominations practised there, it has always been a comfort to me to think that it is not the sepulchre of my dear Lord which is thus desecrated.' This audience appears to have taken place during Gobat's stay as the guest of the king in 1846 (*Samuel Gobat*, 211–12). See, in similar vein, C.R. Conder, *Tent Work in Palestine: A Record of Discovery and Adventure* (London: Richard Bentley, 1878), 371.

[27] *Samuel Gobat*, 367.

[28] The Holy Sepulchre is situated within the Old City, not far from Jaffa Gate.

is widely agreed that, at the time of the Crucifixion, the site of the
Holy Sepulchre lay outside the city walls of Jerusalem and, very
soon afterwards, was incorporated in the city following the construction of an additional wall. This may shed light on an otherwise
puzzling assertion in the second-century 'Paschal Homily' of Melito
of Sardis, in which he four times accuses the Jewish people of having
killed their 'Lord' in the middle of Jerusalem (lines 505–507, 692,
694, 704–706).[29] As a skilled orator, Melito knew how to create
dramatic effect, so that his locating of the Crucifixion in the middle
of Jerusalem could plausibly be put down to rhetorical striving.[30]
He also accuses the Jews a couple of times of having 'killed your
Lord at the great feast' (line 565; cf. line 677),[31] which again does
not miss the opportunity for pathos. However, in the last of the city
references Melito is more explicit: 'But now, in the middle of the
street and in the middle of the city, at the middle of the day for all to
see, there has occurred the unjust killing of a just man' (lines 704–
706). Even here he is striving for rhetorical effect with 'middle of the
street ... middle of the city ... middle of the day', and it is just possible that he is merely making the point that 'this thing was not done
in a corner' (cf. Acts 26:26).

Nevertheless, this location of the Crucifixion is clearly at odds
with the Gospels' tradition, and yet it cannot easily be put down to
either ignorance or indifference. Joachim Jeremias thought that
Melito was influenced by the 'navel of the earth' concept,[32] but this
hardly accounts for the precise terms that he uses. The probable
answer to the riddle was pointed out by Anthony Harvey in a short
communication in 1968,[33] for with the building of Agrippa's 'Third
Wall' in AD 41–44 the site of the Holy Sepulchre – to which area
Melito may be referring – was no longer outside the Jerusalem city
walls. Further speculation about Melito's reference centres on his
use of the word *plateia*, which can mean 'square', in which case he
could be 'reflecting a rather precise tradition that in his time the site
of the Crucifixion was believed to lie in the centre of an open space
in the middle of Aelia Capitolina'.[34] The use of the word also recalls

---

[29] For text see S.G. Hall (ed.), *Melito of Sardis: On Pascha and Fragments*
(Oxford Early Christian Texts; Oxford: Clarendon, 1979), 38, 52.

[30] Cf. J. Murphy-O'Connor, 'Pre-Constantinian Christian Jerusalem', in
A. O'Mahony (ed.), with G. Gunner and K. Hintlian, *The Christian Heritage in the Holy Land* (London: Scorpion Cavendish, 1995), 13–21(18–
19).

[31] See Hall, *Melito of Sardis*, 42, 50.

[32] *Golgotha* (ΑΓΓΕΛΟΣ 1; Leipzig: Eduard Pfeiffer, 1926), 40.

[33] A.E. Harvey, 'Melito and Jerusalem', *JTS* NS 17 (1966), 401–404.

[34] Biddle, *The Tomb of Christ*, 62.

Revelation 11:7–8 and the two witnesses killed by the beast from the bottomless pit, whose bodies lie 'in the street (*plateia*) of the great city which is called spiritually Sodom and Egypt, where also their Lord was crucified' (v. 8).[35] Although this is not at all a direct statement about the Crucifixion, the connection is made, and it is conceivable that the Apocalypse also reflects the situation after AD 41–44 when it was known that the location of Golgotha was now within the city walls. If, as is possible, Melito has been influenced by this text, then the significance of his supposed acquaintance with Jerusalem topography for his reference to the Crucifixion could be impaired. However, his dependence upon Revelation 11:7–8 is difficult to prove and, as we have just noted, it is even possible that the biblical text itself reflects awareness of the change in the relative position of the site of the Crucifixion – which would have altered with the building of the 'Third Wall' if it had been anywhere in the vicinity of the present Church of the Holy Sepulchre. Just over a century after Melito, Eusebius notes in his *Onomastikon* (74:19–21; 75:20–22) that Golgotha 'is pointed out (*deiknutai*) in Aelia to the north of Mount Zion', which approximates to the area in which the Church of the Holy Sepulchre is situated.

The probability that Melito's 'Paschal Homily' reflects a situation in which the site of Golgotha was no longer 'outside the city wall' prompts a question about the Gospel narratives themselves, for if Agrippa's 'Third Wall' was responsible for the change in the relative position of Golgotha then, on almost any understanding of the process of the Gospels' formation, Golgotha was *inside* the city at the time the several Gospels were written.[36] This would have been known to some at least of the evangelists, and probably to some of their earliest readers.

In such circumstances what should a writer of a Gospel do? A statement pointing out that the relative position of Golgotha had altered would be appropriate, but could have been considered intrusive in a story of such gravity; and in any case such a statement, even if appropriate, was not provided. The alternative would be restraint in referring to Golgotha as 'the outside place', and it is interesting to look at the Gospels' references in this light. The data can be summarized easily. According to Matthew, when the soldiers had left off mocking Christ they 'led him away' to be crucified,

---

[35] It seems incontestable that the historical city of Jerusalem underlies this reference, whatever further (symbolical) significance attaches to the 'great city'.

[36] The original outer wall would have been left standing even when superseded by Agrippa's construction, as Professor A.R. Millard has pointed out to me.

and it was 'as they were going out' that they met Simon of Cyrene and forced him to carry the cross (27:31–32). Mark uses similar language and notes that Simon was 'on his way in from the country' (15:21), which implies something about the direction in which the execution party was proceeding. Luke talks of 'leading away' (23:26), while John says that he 'went out' (19:17), adding the significant comment that the place of execution was 'near the city' (v. 20). There is also the one reference of importance outside the Gospels, in Hebrews 13:12: 'Jesus ... suffered outside the gate.'

None of this casts any doubt on the location of Christ's crucifixion, and such executions would in any case have been performed outside the city walls. Nor would it be altogether appropriate to describe these references as 'restrained', simply because they avoid saying that it was *outside the city* that the crucifixion party was headed. On the other hand, it has long been thought that a synoptic variation within the 'Parable of the Tenants' relates to the detail of the crucifixion of Christ. In the Markan version the son of the vineyard owner was killed by the tenants and thrown out of the vineyard (12:8), but the order of events is reversed in Matthew and Luke, according to whom the killing takes place only after the son has been expelled from the vineyard (Mt. 21:39; Lk. 20:15). Is it possible that the difference between Mark on the one hand and Matthew and Luke on the other reflects a change in the position of Golgotha in relation to the outer wall of Jerusalem, following the building of the 'Third Wall'? Whatever our conclusions on these matters, the fact remains that it is the demands of the 'anti-typology' of Hebrews 13:12 that occasion the most straightforward statement in the New Testament about the site of the Crucifixion.

Hills, Hymns and Hyperbole

As we have noted, the idea that Golgotha was a hill or mountain took root quite early; and Christian tradition, piety and hymnology have been diligent in building on the mountain tradition of Golgotha. Somewhere along the line the impulses of 'Sacred Geography' come into play, encapsulating the spiritual and cosmic significance of Golgotha for Christian faith. Christ himself spoke of his being 'lifted up' (Jn 12:32) and drawing humanity to him on the cross. With such a thought in mind, Melito says that it was a 'tall tree' on which the Christ was raised.[37] This is the cross of John Bowring's hymn, 'In the cross of Christ I glory, towering o'er the

---

[37] *On Pascha*, line 707.

wrecks of time.'[38] The Johannine theology of glorification through the cross represents a transformation of the significance otherwise of crucifixion (cf. Jn 12:23–24; 13:31–32), as does Colossians 2:15, where inversion and transformation reach their peak: the shamed Crucified makes a public spectacle of the 'powers and authorities' and processes in triumph over them on the cross. The magnificent verse in the Hupton-Neale hymn, 'Come, ye faithful, raise the anthem', may have found inspiration in Colossians 2:15:

> Ere He raised the lofty mountains,
> formed the sea, or built the sky,
> love eternal, free, and boundless,
> forced the Lord of life to die,
> lifted up the Prince of princes
> on the throne of Calvary.[39]

The literal hill-mountain language is scattered throughout Christian hymnology, perhaps most famously in Cecil Frances Alexander's, 'There is a green hill far away, without a city wall', one of the fourteen compositions in her *Hymns for Little Children* which sought to explain elements of the Apostles' Creed for the benefit of young people like her godsons, who had complained that the Creed was difficult to understand. In this case the hymn has the superscription, 'Suffered under Pontius Pilate, was crucified, dead, and buried.'[40] Since *Hymns for Little Children* was published in 1848, there is little likelihood of what later became known as Gordon's Calvary having influenced the wording.[41] Nor, contrary to common opinion, is it certain that Mrs Alexander was inspired by the walled city of Londonderry and the green hills beyond. When *Hymns for Little Children* was published she was living at Milltown House, Strabane, about fourteen miles from Londonderry, was not yet married to William Alexander, who later became Bishop of Derry, and was therefore not yet resident in the episcopal palace in Londonderry.[42]

---

[38] This hymn was written in 1825 by Sir John Bowring (1792–1872), one-time governor of Hong Kong.

[39] Words by Job Hupton (1762–1849) and John Mason Neale (1818–66).

[40] For the story of Mrs Alexander and her hymn-writing see E. Lovell, *A Green Hill Far Away: The Life of Mrs C.F. Alexander* (Dublin: APCK/London: SPCK, 1970).

[41] On the other hand, Conder quotes the Alexander hymn in *Tent Work*: 'Thus to "a green hill far away, beside (*sic*) a city wall," we turn from the artificial rocks and marble slabs of the monkish Chapel of Calvary' (374).

[42] See Lovell, *A Green Hill Far Away*, 26. William Alexander was Bishop of Derry from 1867 to 1895, and subsequently became Archbishop of Armagh.

Adam and Golgotha

Other significances were found for Golgotha in the development of
a rich and creative Christian tradition. One such, reported by
Origen as being originally 'Hebrew', has it that Golgotha was so
named because Adam's skull was buried there.[43] Early Christian
writers were happy to exploit the theological potential in the tradition. Origen himself, with his universalist tendencies, turned naturally to 1 Corinthians 15:22: 'For as in Adam all die, so in Christ
will all be made alive.' Pseudo-Athanasius saw a deeper significance
in Ephesians 5:14 ('Awake, O sleeper, and rise from the dead, and
Christ will shine on you') which he, with others, took to be
addressed to Adam.[44] So did Paula and Eustochium, adherents of
Jerome, who report also the tradition that the blood of Christ on the
cross trickled down on to Adam's skull, this symbolizing the
washing away of the sins of the first man (the 'protoplastus').[45]
Jerome also notes the Adam-Golgotha tradition when commenting
on Ephesians 5:14.[46] However, the more hard-headed biblical
scholar in him rejects the connection with Adam: in his commentary
on Matthew 27:33 he attributes the name 'Golgotha' to the fact that
criminals were beheaded in the area. Golgotha-Calvary was therefore the place of the beheaded (*decollatorum*).[47] He too, nonetheless, found theological significance in this, in that 'where sin
increased, grace increased all the more' (Rom. 5:20). It is interesting
that Jerome, while repudiating the Adam connection, appeals
to Romans 5:20 and therefore, if but indirectly, to the 'federal
theology' of the Adam-Christ polarity outlined in Romans 5:12–19

---

[43] Origen, *In Matt.* on 27:32 (*PG* 13, col. 1777; it is in the Catena quotation in the footnote that the reference to Hebrew tradition is found). For
texts making the Adam-Golgotha connection see Wilson, 'Golgotha and
the Holy Sepulchre', *PEFQS* 1902, 66–77(67–68, 71–77). See also
Wilson, *Golgotha*, 2–4, 159–66; Jeremias, *Golgotha*, 34–40; Joan E.
Taylor, *Christians and the Holy Places: The Myth of Jewish-Christian
Origins* (Oxford: Clarendon, 1993), 122–34.
[44] *De Passione* 12 (*PG* 28, cols. 207–208).
[45] *Ep. Paulae et Eustochii ad Marcellam* 46 (*PL* 22, col. 485). The letter is
included among Jerome's letters as number 46.
[46] *In Ephes.* on 5:14 (*PL* 26, col. 526).
[47] *In Matt.* on 27:33 (*PL* 26, col. 209). Jerome goes on to note that, according to the Old Testament, Adam was buried at Hebron. This, however, is
an error which he himself helped to create, since he misunderstood
hā'ādām in Joshua 14:15 as a proper noun, so producing the Vulgate
misrendering: 'Adam maximus ibi inter Enacim situs est' ('There among
the Enacim the great Adam is placed').

(cf. 1 Cor. 15:21–22, 44b–49). What we have in these Christian interpretations of the Adam-Golgotha link is, of course, another harking back to Eden, though not now as idyll, as in the Old Testament texts considered in an earlier chapter.[48] The early theologians of the church, moreover, elaborate the Pauline 'federal theology' in such a way as to include Adam personally in the redemptive work of Christ – something that is not explicitly done in the New Testament. Others, like Tatian and the Encratites, denied that Adam was included within the scope of Christ's atonement.[49]

The Centre of the Earth

Our study of Golgotha resurrects another theme discussed earlier. For several centuries, and perhaps with a sideswipe at the claims of classical sites such as Delphi, Jerusalem had been described by Jewish writers as the centre, and then the omphalos, of the land of Israel and even of the entire world.[50] In a number of Christian writers, from quite early on, this idea is transferred to Golgotha, or is associated with Jerusalem as the place of the Crucifixion: Golgotha is the mid-point of the earth.[51] Thus Cyril of Jerusalem in the fourth century talks of Christ extending his arms on the cross in order to embrace the ends of the earth, 'for this Golgotha is the mid-point of the earth'.[52] For Pseudo-Tertullian Golgotha is the centre of the earth, the place where victory was won.[53] Omphalos language is used by Sophronius of Jerusalem (c. 560–638) when in his 'Anacreontica' he refers to the 'sacred navel and rock' of Golgotha.[54] According to the *Annals* of Eutychius of Alexandria (early tenth century), Adam gave instructions that his body be

---

[48] See ch. 2.

[49] Cf. Irenaeus, *Adversus omnes Haereses* 1:28.

[50] See ch. 3.

[51] See Jeremias, *Golgotha*, 40–45; Dorothea R. French, 'Journeys to the Center of the Earth: Medieval and Renaissance Pilgrimages to Mount Calvary', in Barbara N. Sargent-Baur (ed.), *Journeys Toward God: Pilgrimage and Crusade* (Occasional Studies Series, 5; Kalamazoo, MI: SMC XXX Medieval Institute Publications, Western Michigan University, 1992), 45–81.

[52] *Catechesis* 13:28 (*PG* 33, col. 805).

[53] *Adversus Marcionem* 2:4 (*PL* 2, col. 1067).

[54] *Anacreontica* 20 (*PG* 87:3, col. 3820): 'And prostrate I will kiss the sacred navel-point [of the earth], the Rock in which was fixed the tree which undid the curse of the tree.' A fairly free rendering is given by J. Wilkinson, *Jerusalem Pilgrims Before the Crusades* (Warminster: Aris and Phillips, 1977), 91.

buried at the middle of the earth, 'for thence shall come my salvation and the salvation of all my children'.[55] This recalls Psalm
74:12, which is quoted already by Cyril of Jerusalem[56] in the same
connection: 'But God is my king of old, working salvation in the
midst of the earth.'[57] Psalm 74:12 continued to be quoted by Christian writers in connection with the location of Golgotha at the
centre of the earth,[58] and right up to modern times this idea has been
perpetuated in the vase supposedly representing the earth's mid-
point, standing in the Greek Church of the Holy Sepulchre.[59] Thus
the tradition of Golgotha as 'mountain' is complemented by
another that was also first associated with Jerusalem itself:
Golgotha represents the centre or navel of the earth.

So Golgotha enjoys a Zion-like centrality in Christian theology
that leaves literal, physical considerations far behind. Hilary of
Poitiers, in the fourth century, would certainly agree. Hilary
declared that the cross stood not only at the centre of the world but
also at the summit of the universe, so that all the nations might
equally have access to the knowledge of God.[60] Similarly, Andrew
of Crete (c. 660–740) compared the Saviour on the cross, placed at
the centre of the world, with the sun at its height shedding its rays on
the earth.[61] 'Sacred Geography' thus becomes a mechanism
whereby the doctrines associated with Golgotha-Calvary are given
their due prominence. In his book *Holy City, Holy Places?* Peter
Walker treats two prominent theologians of the fourth century,
Eusebius of Caesarea and Cyril of Jerusalem, and their somewhat
contrasting approaches to the exposition of Christian doctrine.[62] In

---

[55] *Annales* 17–19 (cf. 44, 48) (*PG* 111, cols. 911, 917, 918).

[56] *Catechesis* 13:28 (*PG* 33, col. 805).

[57] Those who so used Psalm 74 may have reflected that it was composed
against the background of the destruction of Jerusalem, and that v. 12 was
unlikely to be referring to localized acts of deliverance at the 'city of God'
in the manner of, say, Psalm 48.

[58] Cf., for the late seventh century, Arculf line 13 (text in T. Tobler and A.
Molinier [eds.], *Itinera Hierosolymitana et Descriptiones Terrae Sanctae*
[Publications de la Société de l'Orient Latin, Série Géographique I–II.
Itinera Latina, I; Geneva: J.-G. Fick, 1879], 156–57). For other references
see W. Simpson, 'The Middle of the World, in the Holy Sepulchre', *PEFQS*
1888, 260–63.

[59] Cf. Simpson, 'The Middle of the World', 260–61.

[60] *Comm. in Matt.* 33:4 (*PL* 9, cols. 1073–74).

[61] *Oratio* 9 (*PG* 97, col. 1044).

[62] P.W.L. Walker, *Holy City, Holy Places?: Christian Attitudes to Jerusalem and the Holy Land in the Fourth Century* (Oxford Early Christian
Studies; Oxford: Clarendon, 1990); idem, 'Jerusalem and the Holy Land

Eusebius' theology, revelation and theophany are paramount, even to the extent of an apparent down-playing of what might be called the 'theology of the cross'.[63] It is, then, consistent with this approach that Eusebius, voluminous writer though he was, makes little contribution to our discussion of the 'Sacred Geography' of Golgotha. Cyril, on the other hand, places more emphasis on redemptive aspects of the incarnation, and for him the locus of the Crucifixion has a correspondingly higher place in his writings. This distinction between the two worthies may be valid, provided that allowance is made for the fact that Eusebius' attitudes were formed in the decades preceding the Constantinian annexation of Jewish and Christian holy places in Palestine, while Cyril will have been influenced by his daily acquaintance with the services in the Golgotha buildings complex.[64]

---

[62] (*continued*) in the 4th Century', in O'Mahony (ed.), *The Christian Heritage in the Holy Land*, 22–34(32–34).

[63] Walker, *Holy City*, 256. Walker (66–67) also notes Eusebius' lack of interest in eschatology.

[64] Cf. J. Wilkinson, 'Christian Pilgrims in Jerusalem during the Byzantine Period', *PEQ* 108 (1976), 75–101(91). See also the comments by R.L. Wilken, *The Land Called Holy: Palestine in Christian History and Thought* (New Haven: Yale University Press, 1992), 291n. 27.

Chapter Six

Future Dimensions

If Christian tradition has attributed to Golgotha characteristics that belonged to the historical Jerusalem/Zion as depicted in biblical and post-biblical Jewish tradition, that does not alter the fact that the Old Testament has constructed its view of the *future* city in similar terms, or that these were augmented by other such pictures, relating to both city and land, in the Old Testament and in subsequent Jewish tradition.

Jerusalem 'Above'

If a psalmist could hail the Zion of his day as 'beautiful for elevation' (Ps. 48:3[2]), it is not surprising that in prophetic visions of the future the 'hill of the Lord's house' could be envisaged as towering over all other hills in the vicinity, and indeed throughout the earth. Isaiah and Micah have the same prediction and in almost identical words:

> In days to come[1]
> the mountain of the Lord's house will be established
> as the chief among the mountains,
> exalted above the hills;
> and all the nations will flow to it.
>
> (Isa. 2:2; cf. Mic. 4:1).

Here are combined the ideas of holy mountain and the end-time pilgrimage of the nations to Jerusalem.[2] The Greek Septuagint

---

[1] For the translation of MT *b'ḥryt hymym* in this way see M.A. Sweeney, *Berit Olam: Studies in Hebrew Narrative and Poetry. The Twelve Prophets*, II (Collegeville: Liturgical Press, 2000), 378, comparing the Akkadian *ina aḥrât ūmī*, 'in future days'.

[2] On the subject of pilgrimage to Jerusalem see: E.H. Merrill, 'Pilgrimage and Procession: Motifs of Israel's Return', in A. Gileadi (ed.), *Israel's Apostasy and Restoration: Essays in Honor of Roland K. Harrison* (Grand

translator of Isaiah changed 'flow' to 'come', though evidently not just because he balked at the idea of the antigravitational flow implied in the nations' 'streaming' to the lofty peak, since, in the couple of other places where the Hebrew talks about peoples 'flowing', the Greek again paraphrases.[3] In Isaiah the poem is well suited to its context, for in the following verses there is much emphasis on the abasement of all that is high in human pretensions. In the coming day 'the Lord alone will be exalted' (2:17). Contextual considerations also apply in Micah, though in a different way. The section immediately preceding denounces the leaders of Judah and warns that, because of their misdeeds, Jerusalem will be reduced to rubble and 'the hill of the house' will become 'a mound overgrown with thickets' (3:12, *NIV*). In the section immediately following 4:1–4 the rule of God in Zion is celebrated (vv. 6–8).

---

[2] *(continued)* Rapids: Baker, 1988), 261–72; T.L. Donaldson, 'Proselytes or "Righteous Gentiles"? The Status of Gentiles in Eschatological Pilgrimage Patterns of Thought', *JSP* 7 (1990), 3–27; Y. Tsafrir, 'Jewish Pilgrimage in the Roman and Byzantine Periods', *Akten des XII. Internationalen Kongresses für christliche Archäologie* (Jahrbuch für Antike und Christentum Ergänzungsband, 20, 1; Münster: Aschendorffsche Verlagsbuchhandlung, 1995), 369–76. For Christian pilgrimage to Jerusalem see J. Wilkinson, 'Jewish Holy Places and the Origins of Christian Pilgrimage', in R. Ousterhout (ed.), *The Blessings of Pilgrimage* (Illinois Byzantine Studies, 1; Urbana and Chicago: University of Illinois Press, 1990), 41–53; Dorothea R. French, 'Journeys to the Center of the Earth: Medieval and Renaissance Pilgrimages to Mount Calvary', in Barbara N. Sargent-Baur (ed.), *Journeys Toward God: Pilgrimage and Crusade* (Occasional Studies Series, 5; Kalamazoo, MI: SMC XXX Medieval Institute Publications, Western Michigan University, 1992), 45–81; *eadem,* 'Mapping Sacred Centers: Pilgrimage and the Creation of Christian Topographies in Roman Palestine', *Akten des XII. Internationalen Kongresses für christliche Archäologie* (Jahrbuch für Antike und Christentum Ergänzungsband, 20, 2; Münster: Aschendorffsche Verlagsbuchhandlung, 1995), 792–97; Wendy Pullan, 'Mapping Time and Salvation: Early Christian Pilgrimage to Jerusalem', in G.D. Flood (ed.), *Mapping Invisible Worlds* (Cosmos 9; Edinburgh: Edinburgh University Press, 1993), 23–40; R.L. Wilken, 'Christian Pilgrimage to the Holy Land', in Nitza Rosovsky (ed.), *City of the Great King: Jerusalem from David to the Present* (Cambridge, MA: Harvard University Press, 1996), 117–35.

[3] In the parallel passage in Micah 4:1 the Septuagint has *kai speusousin* ('and will hasten'), which could represent a *Vorlage* with *wmhrw* instead of *wnhrw*. At Jeremiah 51(LXX 28):44, where the nations will no longer 'stream' to the god Bel in Babylon, the Greek has 'will not be assembled (sc. to Babylon)'.

This elevation of Zion is primarily a way of representing through physical geography the supremacy of God and his rule throughout the world. At the same time, the raising up of Zion as God's holy mountain implies his superiority over all other gods and their holy mountains. At first it may seem that this is to read too much into the poem, since Zion will be exalted above other mountains and hills, and a conscious contrast with other *holy* mountains is not immediately obvious. There are, however, a couple of good reasons for foregrounding the idea, implicit in the poem, of God's superiority over the gods of the nations.

First, the uncommon use of the verb *nāhar* to describe the nations 'flowing' to Mount Zion has a parallel in Jeremiah 51:44, where God says, 'I will visit Bel in Babylon and will remove what he has swallowed from his mouth, and nations will no longer flow (*ynhrw*) to him.'[4] The picture of nations 'flowing' or, as we might say, 'streaming' to Babylon to pay homage to Bel no doubt represents an Israelite's view of the dominance of Babylon and its religion in the sixth century when Neo-Babylonian imperial power ensured an enhanced status for the gods of Babylon. Such power and prestige, however, could remain only an aspiration for lowly Judah, and so in Isaiah 2 and Micah 4 the prospect of worldwide devotion to the God of Israel forms part of the prophetic vision of the days to come.

Secondly, the poem in Micah 4 has extra lines, and although it is disputed which version of the poem – the Isaian or the Mican – came first,[5] these lines provide insight into the interpretative thrust of the poem at a very early stage. The picture of future bliss in the Mican version includes the prosperity motif of people sitting under their own vines and fig-trees without fear of molestation, since God has decreed that it should be so (v. 4). What follows in verse 5, beginning with *kî* ('for, because, although'), is in part explanatory:

---

[4] The Septuagint has no mention of Bel in this verse: the nations simply 'flow' to Babylon in the Greek. However, there is no special reason to favour the shorter reading, which may have arisen by haplography. The Greek text of Jeremiah in general may be more troubled by haplography than has usually been appreciated (cf. J.R. Lundbom, *Jeremiah 1–20: A New Translation with Introduction and Commentary* [AB 21A; New York: Doubleday, 1999], 61–62, 885–87; A.G. Shead, *The Open Book and the Sealed Book: Jeremiah 32 in its Hebrew and Greek Recensions* [SJSOT 347; London: Sheffield Academic Press, 2002], 249–50). Verse 44 has the first of three occurrences in the chapter of the verb *pqd*, used of visitation upon the *idols* of Babylon (cf. vv. 47, 52).

[5] Cf. B.S. Childs, *Isaiah* (Old Testament Library; Louisville: Westminster John Knox, 2001), 28.

For all the peoples *walk* each in the name of their gods,
but we will *walk* in the name of the Lord our God forever.

So, in its Mican form, the poem about the holy hill of Zion has to do directly with the true worship of God over against the polytheistic practices of other nations. There is obvious leaning on the verb *hālak* ('walk') in the couplet just quoted, and this picks up the earlier verse according to which the God of Israel would teach the nations his ways 'so that we may walk (*hālak*) in his paths' (v. 2).

Another feature of the poem involves to a degree the supersession of literal, physical geography by 'Sacred Geography'. In its vision of the end-time, Zion assumes the role of Mount Sinai at the time of the exodus: it is from Zion that the *torah* of the Lord will go forth (Isa. 2:3; Mic. 4:2).[6] This absorption of Sinai by Zion is complemented in Isaiah 4:5–6, where the equivalents of the cloud and fire that accompanied Israel through the desert (cf. Exod. 13:21), and that enveloped Mount Sinai at the giving of the law (Exod. 19:16, 18), are recreated on Mount Zion.[7] Now, however, Zion is to function, not just in relation to the people of Israel, but for all the earth, and God's word will adjudicate among the nations to secure an end to war and the establishment of lasting peace (Isa. 2:4).

It would be reasonable to assume that the biblical depictions of end-time pilgrimages to Jerusalem, as in the poem, were, at least partly, constructed from actual experience of such in the historical period. That this is the case is suggested by the correspondence

---

[6] Note that in Numbers 10:33 Sinai is described as the 'mountain of the Lord'. The large Qumran scroll of Isaiah (1QIsa[a]) omits the words 'to the mountain of the Lord' in 2:3, probably by haplography, and has 'that they may teach us' for 'that he (sc. the Lord) may teach us'. If 'they' is not simply a generalizing plural, the reference may be to the teaching role of the priesthood (cf. Mal. 2:7). Pulikottil argues that the omission and change are deliberate, in order to open up a teaching role for the Qumran community, which had no use for the geographical location ('the mountain of the Lord'), but could reinterpret 'the house of the God of Jacob' in a self-interested way. Pulikottil supports this by translating *tṣ'* in the Qumran text by 'has departed/proceeded', which translation does not, however, do justice to the tense of the verb or to the emphatic position of 'from Zion' – 'for from Zion instruction will proceed' (i.e. as distinct from Sinai, the original mountain of the law-giving) (P. Pulikottil, *Transmission of Biblical Texts in Qumran: The Case of the Large Isaiah Scroll 1QIsa*[a] [Journal for the Study of the Pseudepigrapha Supplement Series, 34; Sheffield: Sheffield Academic Press, 2001], 144, 146, 173).

[7] Cf. J.P. Schultz, 'From Sacred Space to Sacred Object to Sacred Person in Jewish Antiquity', *Shofar* 12 (1993), 28–37(31).

between Psalm 122, one of the 'Psalms of Ascents' (Pss. 120–34), and the pilgrimage sections in Isaiah 2 and Micah 4. The association of Psalms 120–34 with pilgrimage to the Jerusalem temple provides the most appropriate life-setting for them. As we read the first verse of Psalm 122 we can easily imagine a community making preparation for the journey to the capital: 'I rejoiced with those who said to me, "Let us go to the house of the Lord."' In Jeremiah 31:5(6), which looks to the reintegration of Israel, sentinels in the hill country of Ephraim are envisaged summoning the population to 'go up to Zion, to the Lord our God'. This expectation is taken further in our two prophetic texts as they envisage non-Israelite peoples encouraging one another to make the journey to the mountain of the Lord (Isa. 2:3; Mic. 4:2). Further, Psalm 122 expresses two of the main themes that inform the prophetic vision, namely justice and peace. The dispensing of justice is implied in the reference to the Davidic thrones of judgment that are set up in Jerusalem (v. 5), while the psalm concludes with heavy emphasis on the topic of peace in relation to Jerusalem (vv. 6–9). In the *prophetic* depiction of the future, however, these two themes are internationalized: 'the law will go out from Zion' and the nations 'will beat their swords into ploughshares' (Isa. 2:3–4; Mic. 4:2–3).

The idea of end-time pilgrimage by the nations to Jerusalem is developed in other prophetic texts such as Isaiah 56:6–8; 66:20–21; Zechariah 8:22–23; 14:16–21. The last-cited speaks specifically of an annual pilgrimage to Jerusalem for the festival of Tabernacles (Zech. 14:16, 18, 19), and may be conceptually closer to our Isaian-Mican poem than appears on the surface. In the poem the nations' coming for the dispensing of the divine Torah is not associated with any calendrical event, but it is easy to see how that this law-giving became associated with Tabernacles. The Deuteronomic stipulation on the septennial reading of the law requires that it be carried out at the festival of Tabernacles 'when all Israel comes to appear before the Lord your God at the place that he will choose' (Deut. 31:9–13[10–11]). This association of Tabernacles with the reading of Torah is instanced in Nehemiah 8. The chapter begins with the Judeans assembling in Jerusalem on the first day of the seventh month to hear Ezra the scribe read from the Book of the Law 'from dawn until noon' (v. 3). This attention to the Book of the Law continued on the second day of the month, during which they read the regulations for the observance of Tabernacles (vv. 14–15). And when Tabernacles came round, they had Ezra read – again! – from the Book of the Law on the seven days of the festival (v. 18). Thus, although the poem in Isaiah-Micah does not mention Tabernacles, and Zechariah 14 has no reference to the Torah, they are evidently showing us facets of the same, developing vision of the end-time.

The vision of nations coming to 'the house of the God of Jacob' then becomes the basis in the Isaian poem for a summons to Judah-Israel in the present: 'Come, O *house of Jacob*, let us walk in the light of the Lord' (2:5). The effect of this challenge, as Childs has noted,[8] is to put Judah-Israel *qua* 'house of Jacob' in the valley of decision – between the nations who come to acknowledge the God of Jacob (vv. 1–4) and the 'house of Jacob' of verses 6–8, abandoned by God because of the idolatries that have filled the land. The readers or hearers of the text are bidden in the present to commit to God in such a way that they themselves anticipate the future submission of the Gentile peoples to Torah; and this they can achieve by renouncing the characteristic Gentile superstitions and idolatries that filled the land at the time of the prophet and that are summarized in verses 6–8.

The physical elevation of Jerusalem/Zion above the surrounding terrain also forms part of the eschatological vision of Zechariah 14:10. The idea is not so clearly expressed here as it is in the Zion poem of Isaiah 2 and Micah 4. Presumably this accounts for the failure of two ancient Bible translations, the Septuagint and the Targum, to represent the notion of elevation in their renderings of the verse. The Septuagint, by misunderstanding the meaning of the MT *yswb* ('will be turned into'), has God 'surrounding' all the land and the desert (*sic*), and then takes the verb *r'mh* ('be raised up') as a proper name ('Rama'). The Targum's not uncharacteristic substitution of 'will be increased'[9] for 'will be raised up' is so far from appreciating the differentiation between Jerusalem and the surrounding plain that, as we shall see, it goes on to suggest that Jerusalem would extend to the Mediterranean coast.

This raising up of Jerusalem comes in a chapter that already describes physical upheaval in the vicinity of Jerusalem, when the Mount of Olives is split in two (v. 4) and fresh water flows from Jerusalem in both easterly and westerly directions (v. 8). The creation of a large plain with Jerusalem at its centre is seen by Meyers and Meyers as the fourth and last in a series of environmental improvements that are the concern of verses 6–11.[10] The relative

---

[8] *Isaiah*, 31.

[9] It is a characteristic of Targumic paraphrasing that certain words (e.g. 'strong/be strong', 'increase') are used for a wide range of underlying Hebrew terms.

[10] C.L. Meyers and E.M. Meyers, *Zechariah 9–14: A New Translation with Introduction and Commentary* (AB 25C; New York: Doubleday, 1993), 441–42, 499–500.

unproductivity of the area will be remedied by this levelling of the contours. At the same time, and somewhat less speculatively, Meyers and Meyers allow that verse 10 is concerned to represent Jerusalem as physically exalted above its immediate surroundings. Indeed, this applies whether we translate *r'mh* by 'will be raised up' (cf. *NIV*) or by something less emphatic like 'shall remain aloft' (*NRSV*).

It is from this Jerusalem, rather than from the temple as in Ezekiel 47 and Joel 4(3), that the 'living water' flows (v. 8). But this is in keeping with the standpoint of the chapter, which envisages the sanctity of the temple reaching out into all Jerusalem and Judah (vv. 20–21).

The Riverine City

This leads appropriately to the 'Riverine City'. First we must look at a present-tense reference in Psalm 46:5–6(4–5) which hyperbolizes on Jerusalem as known to the psalmist. We have already noted verse 5(4) in connection with the river of paradise.[11] A literal translation of the verse might run: 'A river – its streams make glad the city of God, the holy dwelling(s) of the Most High.'[12] The context is of seething waters, the earth in commotion, and the overthrow of nations, themselves sometimes symbolized by waters (cf. Isa. 17:12; Jer. 6:23; Dan. 7:2–3). In part, the picture is of creation undone: the earth gives way, and the mountains fall into the heart of the sea. God's works are 'desolations' of destructive things like spears and shields, and thus does he bring cessation (*mašbît*; cf. the Hebrew word for 'sabbath') to human warring (vv. 9–10[8–9]). Flanked by such references, and strongly contrasting with them, are verses 5–6(4–5) with their idyll of the well-irrigated city of God. As we noted in chapter 4, the historical Jerusalem is not so favoured. H.C. Leupold is representative of those who nevertheless try to square the psalm and the city, seeing the reference to the river and its streams as Isaiah 8:6–8 'recast in more poetic fashion'.[13] He detects a contrast in Isaiah 8 between the mighty river, symbolizing Assyria the world power, and the 'streamlet' running 'from the fountain of Siloam to the east of the holy city', symbolizing the kingdom of God

---

[11] See ch. 1.

[12] R.J. Clifford objects to 'the usual translation' on the ground that it does not fit the context; he himself declines to offer a translation (*The Cosmic Mountain in Canaan and the Old Testament* [Harvard Semitic Monographs, 4; Cambridge, MA: Harvard University Press, 1972], 149–50n. 68).

[13] *Exposition of the Psalms* (London: Evangelical Press, 1972), 365.

as perceived by unbelievers.[14] A different approach to the translation of Psalm 46:5(4) was offered by E.J. Kissane: 'A river whose
streams rejoice the city of God/Is the sanctuary, the dwelling of the
Most High.'[15] His explanation is that, just as a stream irrigates land,
so the temple was conceived as conveying blessing to Israel.[16] It is
arguable, however, that this involves a simple grammatical incon-
gruity since, strictly speaking, it is now the masculine noun 'sanctuary' that is the antecedent of the feminine suffixes in verse 6(5), and
the translation and explanation are therefore questionable.

So we are shut up to a poetic ('mythic') interpretation of Psalm
46:5(4). Most probably it is the tradition of the river of paradise
that has inspired the non-literal image in this verse. With the psalmist's 'streams' or 'channels' we may compare the four 'heads' or
'headwaters' associated with the river of Eden in Genesis 2:10–14.
As we have noted in chapter 1, the connection between Eden and
Zion is actually signed for us in the paradise tradition with the
naming of one of the Eden distributaries after the spring Gihon that,
from outside the city wall, supplied Jerusalem with much of its
water (Gen. 2:13; cf. 2 Chr. 32:30; 33:14). Moreover, if Eden truly
has the characteristics of a sanctuary, as is sometimes suggested,[17]
then the conflation of Eden with Zion – 'the holy place where the
Most High dwells' (Ps. 46:5[4]) – becomes all the more likely.

Several other texts develop the theme of aquatic Zion as they
envisage the future that God has in store for the city. In the vision of
Ezekiel 47:1–12 a river emerges from under the threshold of the
temple and flows down to the Dead Sea, whose waters are rendered
fresh by this infusion. In his vision the prophet is told that a fishing
industry will flourish in the Dead Sea region, and that wondrously
productive fruit trees will grow on the banks of the temple river 'because the water for them issues from the sanctuary' (v. 12).[18] An
ancient near eastern illustration of the idea comes in the form of a
palace relief from eighteenth-century Mari in Mesopotamia, whose
registers depict a temple scene in which streams of water give life to
stylized plants.[19] The transformation of Ezekielan apocalyptic in

---

[14] Isaiah 8 mentions 'the gently flowing waters of Shiloah' (v. 6) and 'the
mighty and great waters of the River (=the Euphrates)' (v. 7).
[15] *The Book of Psalms Translated from a Critically Revised Hebrew Text*, I
(Dublin: Browne and Nolan, 1953), 203.
[16] Kissane's comment on 'God is within it' (v. 6[5]) is, 'The Temple is the
source of blessing' (204).
[17] See ch. 1.
[18] Cf. Psalm 36:9–10(8–9).
[19] Cf. O. Keel, *The Symbolism of the Biblical World: Ancient Near Eastern
Iconography and the Book of Psalms* (tr. T.J. Hallett; New York: Seabury
Press, 1978), 143.

the book of Revelation is illustrated in the way in which the river and trees function in Revelation 22:1–2. The river of the water of life issues from 'the throne of God and of the Lamb' and flows down the middle of the street of the 'Holy City'. The leaves of the tree of life, which stands on either side of the river, are said to be for the healing *of the nations* (v. 2).[20] Such a conception transcends the narrower limits of Ezekiel's vision, in which the fruit of the trees serves as food and their leaves as a source of healing (47:12). For Ezekiel, the beneficiaries are the people of Israel, though, as the next section on the boundaries of the land indicates, they include the resident alien, who is to be treated as a native-born Israelite (47:22).

The closing vision of the book of Joel speaks of Zion as God's holy hill, his place of residence (4:17[3:17]; cf. 4:21[3:21]). It also has a truncated version of the Ezekiel river vision[21] that talks of a fountain gushing forth from the Jerusalem temple and irrigating the wadi of Shittim (or 'Acacias'; 4:18[3:18]). If this is indeed the Wadi-en-Nar that leads down to the Dead Sea,[22] then the parallel with Ezekiel's revivifying waters is the closer. In Zechariah 14:8 a more extended function is envisaged for the 'living water' that is portrayed as flowing from Jerusalem, half in the direction of the Dead Sea and half towards the Mediterranean Sea. There is no specific mention of the temple here. More emphasis is put on the constancy of the water supply, which flows both summer and winter and transcends the seasonal fluctuation of the like of the Kidron. This development is set in the context of God's kingship over the earth (v. 9), which is also the setting for the comparison in Isaiah 33 of future Zion with 'a place of broad rivers and streams', where, however, there would be no galleys or great ships because the superior power of God would not tolerate them (v. 21).[23]

The Spread of Holiness

The Zion of the future will live out its vocation to be God's 'holy hill', according to various prophetic texts (cf. Isa. 11:9; 56:7; Zech. 8:3). In addition, the idea that this holiness would extend beyond its

---

[20] Cf. D.I. Block, *The Book of Ezekiel: Chapters 25–48* (Grand Rapids/ Cambridge: Eerdmans, 1998), 696–97, on Ezekiel's river as of national rather than cosmic significance.

[21] Since there are scarcely any internal clues to the dating of the book of Joel it is not automatically assumed that Ezekiel predates it.

[22] Cf. H.W. Wolff, *Joel and Amos* (Hermeneia; Philadelphia: Fortress, 1977), 83.

[23] Or, if they had military significance, because they would not be necessary in the new order.

normal confines is developed in surprising ways in the last two verses of Zechariah 14 (vv. 20–21). First it is said that 'the bells of the horses' will bear the legend 'Holy to the Lord' (v. 20). The suggestion is startling because this sets up a direct comparison with the inscription on the gold plate of the high priest's diadem as described in Exodus 28:36. Holy 'mount' indeed! '[I]t is difficult to see what horses', says Monsignor Ronald Knox in a footnote to his translation of verse 20.[24] We are not told anything more about them, and Meyers and Meyers take them as symbolizing war, since horses appear principally in military contexts.[25] In Zechariah 9–14 horses are twice mentioned in connection with enemy attack on Jerusalem, and in both cases as sharing the divinely inflicted judgment on the attacking forces (12:4; 14:15). If, then, the horses are 'emblazoned' with 'Holy to the Lord', war and warfare must truly be at an end. However, it is not necessary to limit the significance of the horses in this way. By verse 20 the theme of the end-time pilgrimage is well under way, and the horses fit comfortably into this picture. The military (horses *and* chariots) and pilgrimage themes also combine in Isaiah 66:20, where the exiles of Judah are brought back to the holy mountain in Jerusalem 'on horses, in chariots and wagons, and on mules and camels'.

The extension of the divine holiness affects even the service-ware of the temple and of the domestic dwellings of Jerusalem and Judah, according to Zechariah 14:20b–21. First it is said that the temple cooking pots in use in the temple court area will be like the sacred bowls in front of the altar. The altar in question must be the altar of incense in the temple, and the 'bowls' will be those used in blood rituals associated with this altar. In terms of 'graded holiness', therefore, the outside cooking pots have stepped up a class. Next it is envisaged that the ordinary pots in use in Jerusalem and Judah will become 'holy' and will be usable by those who come to offer sacrifice at the temple. While the text says that such pots will be 'holy to the Lord of hosts', and not that they will be inscribed after this fashion, the previous mention of inscriptions on horse-bells and the discovery on a number of Palestinian sites of pots with the letters *q-d-š* ('holiness', 'holy') incised on them make this a possibility.[26] The inscribed pots that archaeology has brought to light appear to have been used originally for common purposes and then

---

[24] *The Holy Bible: A Translation from the Latin Vulgate in the Light of the Hebrew and Greek Originals* (London: Burns and Oates, 1949).

[25] Meyers and Meyers, *Zechariah 9–14*, 480.

[26] Cf. R.P. Gordon, 'Inscribed Pots and Zechariah XIV 20–1', *VT* 42 (1992), 120–23.

subsequently to have been earmarked for special service. Or, as Zechariah 14:21 puts it,

> Every pot in Jerusalem and Judah will be holy to the Lord of hosts, and all those who offer sacrifice will come and use them and cook with them ...

As with the horse bells, it is a fair question why pots lowly and not so lowly should merit special notice at the climax of the 'vision' of Zechariah 14. The communication and extension of the realm of the holy is without doubt a factor, though holiness is not a conspicuous interest of either Zechariah 9–14 or the earlier chapters of the book. Again, the end-time pilgrimage theme is undoubtedly influential, in that the survivors of the nations are expected to come to Jerusalem at festival time – we might compare the nations 'streaming' to Zion in Isaiah 2/Micah 4 – and special provision for their worship is required. What is clear is that the last two verses of the book of Zechariah have inverted that view of holiness represented in the companion prophecy of Haggai, where communicability is associated with uncleanness and *in*communicability with holiness (Hag. 2:10–14).[27]

Extended Boundaries

The Old Testament describes at length the military achievements and the territorial gains associated with David the founder of the Judean dynasty, and the subsequent tradition by and large holds as aspirational a return to the territorial dimensions of the Davidic empire and the establishment of a 'Greater Israel'. This 'Greater Israel' concept is sometimes invoked to explain the principle of selection by which Amos targets the neighbouring states denounced in Amos 1–2, and also the reference to the restoration of the 'fallen booth of David' in Amos 9:11–12.[28]

Zechariah 9:1–7 is a special passage as far as this 'Greater Israel' concept is concerned.[29] Here the prophet's eye ranges across the

---

[27] Cf. D.J.A. Clines, 'Sacred Space, Holy Places and Suchlike', in *On the Way to the Postmodern: Old Testament Essays, 1967–1998. Volume II* (SJSOT 293; Sheffield: Sheffield Academic Press, 1998), 542–54(550–51).

[28] See M.E. Polley, *Amos and the Davidic Empire: A Socio-Historical Approach* (New York/Oxford: Oxford University Press, 1989), 70–74. The origin of Amos 9:11–12 is much debated, but the aspirational character of the verses remains, regardless of provenance.

[29] See P.D. Hanson, 'Zechariah 9 and the Recapitulation of an Ancient Ritual Pattern', *JBL* 92 (1973), 37–59.

Syrian, Phoenician and Philistine homelands and announces what
will befall them. There are echoes of the prophetic 'Oracles against
the Nations' in the section, and yet there are supervening elements
uncharacteristic of the standard invective of the genre – just as the
portrayal of Zion's king in the verses immediately following is of a
beneficent victor 'humble and mounted on a donkey' and destined
to proclaim peace to the nations (vv. 9, 10). This more inclusive attitude towards foreign kingdoms may begin with the first verse of the
chapter, depending on how we translate it. Two modern versions
represent the possibilities:

> The word of the Lord is in the land of Hadrach;
> it alights on Damascus,
> for, no less than all the tribes of Israel,
> the capital of Aram belongs to the Lord. (*REB*)

> The word of the Lord is against the land of Hadrach
> and will rest upon Damascus –
> for the eyes of all people and all the tribes of Israel
> are on the Lord. (*NIV*)

In the former case Hadrach and Damascus are regarded as existing
within the domain of the God of Israel, and the emended text represented in 'the capital of Aram belongs to the Lord' reinforces the
idea. *NIV*, by contrast, assumes a directly hostile tone: the divine
word that is 'against' Hadrach may be assumed to 'rest' upon
Damascus in a comparably hostile fashion. An inimical sense for the
preposition b^e is possible, nevertheless we might have expected ^cal if
the poet-prophet had intended to say 'against the land of Hadrach'.
Furthermore, the clear implications of verse 7 in relation to the
Philistines would tend to support a non-hostile reference in verse 1.
If that is the case, verse 1 is not so much laying claim to Syrian territory on behalf of Judah-Israel as claiming that it falls under the
sovereign control of the Lord. Ultimately the two approaches to the
verse may amount to much the same. Moreover, if Hadrach, identified with Hatarikka in Assyrian inscriptions, is correctly located to
the south of Aleppo, the claim that God's writ runs this far encompasses rather more territory to the north of Israel than David or
Solomon were ever thought to have controlled.[30]

The Philistines feature in a number of Old Testament texts where
Israelite territorial ambitions are involved. They lived on the

---

[30] Cf. Meyers and Meyers, *Zechariah 9–14*, 92: Hadrach 'lay well beyond
the greatest extent of the Davidic-Solomonic kingdom and thus was not
within either the historical or ideal borders of the Israelite kingdom'.

western flank of Israel and therefore immediately in the path of any Israelite expansion toward the Mediterranean Sea. Here already lies part of the significance of the 'proto-Philistines' of the book of Genesis.[31] The term 'Philistine' is commonly hailed as an anachronism in Genesis, since the Philistines are reckoned to have arrived in Palestine in the twelfth century, as suggested by the apparent mention of them under the name 'Peleset' on the Medinet Habu reliefs of Rameses III of Egypt. However, excessive preoccupation with historical niceties can rob these Genesis Philistines of their proper narrative significance. These 'proto-Philistines' are not altogether friendly neighbours of Abraham and Isaac. By Genesis 26 the rivalry between Isaac and the Gerarites, and the terms in which it is recounted, suggest strongly that what we have is the playing out in an ancient patriarchal context of land issues that were later to see the Philistines of the pentapolis and the Israelites in deadly contest.

This struggle over territory surfaces at various points throughout the remainder of the Old Testament, but since we are concerned with futuristic aspects of the topic we return directly to Zechariah 9. The remarkable thing about the Philistine section in this chapter (vv. 5–7) is the expectation that, when God's acts of judgment have fallen, the Philistine remnant will be treated with great generosity:

> I shall remove the blood from their mouths,
> and their abominations from between their teeth.
> Those who are left will [belong] to our God
> and will be like a clan in Judah,
> and Ekron will become like the Jebusite(s).
>
> (v. 7)

On the one hand, it may be proximity to the Israelite homeland, and indeed the reckoning of Philistine land as properly belonging to Israelite tribal territory, that accounts for this special treatment for Ekron in particular. On the other hand, such proximity would, according to Deuteronomic theology, have qualified the cities of Philistia for subjection to the exterminatory 'ban'[32] – except that the Philistines are notably absent from the biblical lists of Canaanite peoples scheduled for dispossession and worse (e.g. Gen. 15:19–21).[33] So, according to Zechariah 9:7, the Philistines are to be favourably treated, and somewhat in contradistinction to

---

[31] I have briefly discussed this aspect of the biblical Philistines in 'The Ideological Foe: The Philistines in the Old Testament', written for the forthcoming Festschrift in honour of Kevin J. Cathcart.

[32] See Deuteronomy 20:16–17.

[33] See, however, Joshua 13:1–3.

their fate as portrayed by other prophets (cf. Jer. 47:1–7; Ezek. 25:15–17).

However, Zechariah 9:7 also claims that this turn-around will be accompanied by purificatory measures so that the Philistines and their territory are fit for inclusion in the Israelite fold. Philistine uncleanness is represented in their Gentile custom of eating flesh without the blood having been drained off, and of eating what are described as 'abominations'. The prohibition on eating flesh with the blood still in it is associated with Noah in the book of Genesis where, presumably, it is held to be binding on all his descendants (Gen. 9:4); elsewhere in the Old Testament it is typically an Israelite observance (Lev. 17:10–12; 'neither you nor any alien living among you is to consume blood' [v. 12]; Deut. 12:23–25).[34] In Zechariah 9 the prophet foresees a time when Philistines would be relieved of their unclean Gentile habits and would qualify for incorporation in Judah. There is loss of autonomy implied, for Judah and Philistia will not simply co-exist side by side: Judah will absorb Philistia. Nevertheless, the privileged knowledge of the God of Israel will be extended to Israel's old enemy, and Ekron is to be incorporated into the Judean kingdom in just the way that the pre-Israelite Jebus became an Israelite city following its conquest by David (cf. 2 Sam. 5:6–9). The expectation of Zechariah 9:7, therefore, is that Judah would extend its borders westwards to incorporate the land of the Philistines.

The idea of God's sovereignty extending beyond Israelite borders, and of the incorporation of adjacent Philistine land into Israelite territory, is expressed more fully in the ancient Jewish Aramaic version (the Targum) of Zechariah 9 which, in common with the Targum to the Latter Prophets in general, had probably crystallized in something akin to its present shape by the second or third century of the present era. Already in the first verse of the chapter the Targum is engaging in territorialism. Where the MT refers to Damascus as the 'resting-place' of God's word of prophecy – and not necessarily in an inimical sense, as we have already seen – the Targum adjusts the sense: 'and Damascus will again belong to the land of (the house of) his *Shekinah*'. Since Damascus is included among the states listed in 2 Samuel 8 as having become tributary to David (vv. 5–6), the Targumist can think of it *returning* to the Israelite fold at a future date.[35] The 'resting-place' of which the

---

[34] Cf. also the recommendation issued by the 'Jerusalem Council' to Gentile churches in Syria and Cilicia (Acts 15:20, 28–29).

[35] Song of Songs r. 7:5 envisages the expansion of Jerusalem as far as Damascus, on the basis of Zechariah 9:1 ('And Damascus will be his resting-place') read in the light of Psalm 132:14 ('This is my resting-place forever').

Targumist is thinking is, doubtless, that of Psalm 132:8, 14, where Zion is declared to be 'my (sc. God's) resting-place forever' (v. 14; cf. Isa. 66:1). Moreover, the Targum uses the same language as in verse 1, now in reference to Hamath and, apparently, Tyre and Sidon in verse 2: 'Hamath also will again belong to the land of (the house of) his *Shekinah*; Tyre and Sidon, though she was very strong.' Again, in verse 6 the Targum anticipates the MT of verse 7 by introducing the idea of Israelite absorption of a Philistine city into its future kingdom. The MT says that a *mamzēr* will occupy Ashdod, and, whether *mamzēr* refers to an individual or is collective (cf. *NIV* 'Foreigners'), the word appears to be as negatively cast as the clause that follows ('and I will cut off the pride of the Philistines'). The Targum, however, talks of the house of Israel living in Ashdod 'where they were as foreigners'. This probably alludes to the allocation of Ashdod to Judah in Joshua's tribal allotment (Josh. 15:47), and to the reports of the Israelites' failure to annex Ashdod (see Josh. 11:22; 13:1–4).[36]

Since even the MT of verse 7 is talking about the incorporation of parts of Philistia in the community of Judah and its God, the Targum can subscribe enthusiastically. Its 'purification' of the Philistine remnant is more radical, however, in that it says that God will 'destroy those who eat blood and abominations' from among the Philistines. Thereafter it is unhesitantly positive: 'and the *gywryn* who are left among them will also be added to the people of our God and will be like princes of the house of Judah, and Ekron will be filled with the house of Israel like Jerusalem'. Here *gywr* must have its technical sense of 'proselyte'; by this route the Targum, which displays its nationalistic tendencies less favourably elsewhere, is able to match the MT's unusually positive view of the Philistines in the future.

Greater Jerusalem

The idea that not only the Israelite domain but also Jerusalem itself would expand physically in the future is fathered, in post-biblical literature, on a couple of Old Testament texts. 'For you will spread out to the right and to the left, and your descendants will dispossess nations and settle in desolate cities' (Isa. 54:3) is referred directly to Zion by some modern interpreters,[37] while others are equally confident that

---

[36] According to 2 Chronicles 26:6 Uzziah destroyed its walls and (re)built towns in the area.

[37] For example, J.D.W. Watts, *Isaiah 34–66* (WBC 25; Waco: Word Books, 1987), 237.

Jerusalem the city is not addressed in any of the first ten verses of Isaiah 54 (contrast vv. 11–15).[38] Most probably, verse 3 is a poetic statement about enlargement of the post-exilic community rather than an assertion about the extension of the city boundaries of Jerusalem. On the other hand, the Targum's substitution of 'south' and 'north' for 'right' and 'left' slightly intensifies the idea of physical extension of the city which is mentioned already in the Targumic rendering of verse 1. However, for the clearest expression of the idea of the enlargement of Jerusalem on the horizontal plane we have to go to the Midrash on Song of Songs and to the Targum to Zechariah 14:10. We have already looked at Zechariah 14:10 in connection with the theme of the elevation of Zion, but hidden in its Targumic form is also the notion that one day Jerusalem will extend to the Mediterranean coast: 'It will increase and remain in its place, from the Gate of the tribe of Benjamin to the site of the first gate, to the Corner Gate, and [from] the Tower of Hippicus to the king's pits.'

Two features of the last clause are deserving of comment. First, the Targum represents the Tower of Hananel of the MT by the Hippicus Tower built by Herod the Great and, according to Josephus, left intact by the Romans when they destroyed Jerusalem in AD 70.[39] Secondly, for its translation of BH *yqb* ('winepress') the Targum has a unique equivalent based on the noun *šyh*, which denotes an ordinary pit or cavity rather than a winepress. Although there is no other biblical reference to royal winepresses in the vicinity of Jerusalem, there is mention of a royal garden in Nehemiah 3:15; nor, with the prompt of MT Zechariah 14:10, would it have taxed a Targumist's mind too much to imagine the existence of a royal winepress in the Jerusalem area. However, the Targum appears to decline this obvious interpretative possibility, and the Midrash on Song of Songs provides the likely explanation of the Targumic *šyhy*, not only in using the same word but also in explaining that these are 'cavities' hollowed out by God himself: 'up to the pits (*šyhyh*) of Ripa/Yapho, up to the winepresses that the supreme king of kings, the Holy One blessed be he, hollowed out' – in other words, the Mediterranean Sea. Thus, according to both Targum and Midrash, Jerusalem will extend to the Mediterranean coast.[40]

---

[38] Cf. J.F.A. Sawyer, 'Daughter of Zion and Servant of the Lord in Isaiah: A Comparison', *JSOT* 44 (1989), 89–107(94–95).

[39] *War* 7:1.

[40] Cf. R.P. Gordon, '*Terra Sancta* and the Territorial Doctrine of the Targum to the Prophets', in J.A. Emerton and S.C. Reif (eds.), *Interpreting the Hebrew Bible: Essays in honour of E.I.J. Rosenthal* (University of Cambridge Oriental Publications, 32; Cambridge: Cambridge University Press, 1982), 119–31(128–31).

The Targum's singling out of the Hippicus Tower at Zechariah 14:10 has more than one possible explanation. If it is correctly identified in the area of the Jaffa Gate within the Old City of Jerusalem, then it is an appropriate landmark on the west side of the city, whence the city boundary might be envisaged as reaching out west to the Mediterranean coast. At the same time, it is quite likely that, when the text of the Targum to the Prophets was taking shape, Jerusalem had suffered the first, and probably also the second, of its dismantlings by the Romans, in AD 70 and AD 135 respectively. As we have seen, the Herodian towers were among the few constructions left standing by the Romans. The Targum to Zechariah 14:10 would then have significance for this later period rather as Meyer and Meyer suggest in connection with the original Hebrew text of the verse and the surviving landmarks in the city following the *Babylonian* destruction:

> ... if the city walls had not yet been rebuilt or had been only partially restored, the most visible extant architectural remains of greater Jerusalem would be the ones most likely to serve the prophet's purposes in depicting a large and populous city, much bigger than the much-reduced site of the Persian period.[41]

Since in this depiction of Jerusalem as a city reaching to the Mediterranean coast there is no overt interest in the extension *pari passu* of sanctuary-type holiness to the land thus incorporated, the question may be fairly asked whether what we are discussing is just another form of imperialist territorialism. W.D. Davies thinks not, suggesting instead that what is reflected here is the yearning of Jews banished from Jerusalem by the Hadrianic decree, or otherwise living outside the 'holy land', to be counted as living in the holy city. One answer was to find in the Scriptures predictions of the expansion of Jerusalem to include the places where they were then living.[42] This may well be so, not only in the Targum to Zechariah 14:10 but also in the Targumic rendering of elements within Zechariah 9:1–7, as discussed above. How important the concept of holy *land*, if not holy city, became in post-biblical times can be seen in the development of the practice of secondary burial (*ossilegium*) which involved the depositing, back in the land, of the bones of Jews who had died outside the land, so that the departed would suffer no disadvantage on the day of resurrection. At the least, Davies'

---

[41] Meyers and Meyers, *Zechariah 9–14*, 447.
[42] *The Gospel and the Land: Early Christianity and Jewish Territorial Doctrine* (Berkeley: University of California Press, 1974), 232–33, 234–35.

explanation of the much-expanded Jerusalem counsels against unidimensional interpretation of texts that have to do with territorial expansion.[43]

As we have seen, it was expected that even the non-Jewish peoples would come as pilgrims to Jerusalem/Zion when once the ancient promises of deliverance and prosperity were fulfilled. In the meantime there was good reason for exiled Jews, and even for pious Christians, to make their pilgrimage, as chapter 7 describes, to the Jerusalem-that-was.

---

[43] The figure of coastal Jerusalem, but perhaps without indebtedness to the rabbinic idea just discussed, appears in Yehuda Amichai's poem, *Sha'ar Yerushalayim*, which begins, *Yerushalayim 'ir namal 'l sepat hannetsach* ('Jerusalem is a port city on the shore of eternity'). In the poem, the temple mount has the role of a ship. *Sha'ar Yerushalayim* is no. 21 in Amichai's anthology, *Achshav Bara'ash: Shirim 1963–1968* (Tel-Aviv: Schocken, 1971), 19.

Chapter Seven

Marching to Zion[1]

Among the visions of future Jerusalem/Zion that we have just considered is the theme of pilgrimage by nations converted to the worship of the God of Israel. The idea is rooted in the practice of ancient Israel itself, and in truth the 'holy city' has never ceased to be a focus of interest and veneration for Jews and Christians.

The phrase 'Marching to Zion' comes in a version of Isaac Watts's hymn 'Come ye that love the Lord'. Here Watts (1674–1748) depicts the life of faith as a spiritual pilgrimage towards the heavenly Zion. The hymn is typical of many of his compositions in its insistence on joy and celebration as hallmark features of biblical – by which I mean both Jewish and Christian – religion. Watts had set out to provide his congregation at Mark Lane, in London, with new songs of praise more worthy of Christian worship than the dirgeful chants that were its traditional garb.

Pilgrimage was, and is, a feature of the major world religions. The term covers a variety of experiences and endeavours, and may be variously defined. Typically, it involves a journey to a place of religious importance for the fulfilment of a religious purpose, in which prayer and worship are usually prominent. In the Judeo-Christian tradition Jerusalem (or Zion) has been uniquely a focus of pilgrimage for close on three millennia.

Pilgrimage in Temple Times

The Israelites of Old Testament times could make pilgrimage to the central sanctuary – Jerusalem for most of the historical period – for

---

[1] This paper, the full title of which was 'Marching to Zion: The Jerusalem Pilgrimage Theme from the Bible to Byzantium', was read as the Fifth Annual Semitic Studies Lecture at the Institute of Byzantine Studies, The Queen's University, Belfast, on 6 March 2003. It is a pleasure to recall the kindness of Margaret Mullet, Derek Beattie and their colleagues during my visit.

personal reasons such as the performance of cleansing rites (e.g. the Israelite equivalent of 'churching', Lev. 12:6–8) or the fulfilling of vows made in times of stress or crisis. There were, however, the regular occasions when the religiously observant would appear at the house of God to worship in fulfilment of a more general religious obligation. The story of Hannah in 1 Samuel 1–2 brings together both categories, since it is in the course of the annual family visit to Shiloh that Hannah vows to give back to God the son for whom she has been praying.

Marching, or at least walking, to Zion is a religious duty laid upon all male Israelites in the Old Testament. The laws of the Pentateuch include the requirement that three times in the year – the three 'occasions', or $r^e galim$, of the festivals of Passover, Weeks and Tabernacles – adult males should present themselves before God at the central sanctuary (Exod. 23:14; 34:23; Deut. 16:16). However, apart from general injunctions and instructions about sacrifice, the Old Testament has little to say about proceedings at these festivals. This is better appreciated if we contrast the detailed prescriptions given for the ritual of the Day of Atonement (Lev. 16), or the information provided on the Akitu ceremonial during the New Year festivals in Babylon, when Marduk was honoured.[2] Or the whole tractates in the Mishnah devoted to the detail of festival observance.[3] We do have Old Testament descriptions of special observances of Tabernacles in the reign of Solomon (1 Kgs. 8:2), and of Passover in the reigns of Hezekiah and Josiah (2 Kgs. 23:21–23; 2 Chr. 30:1–20; 35:1–19), but again these do not favour us with much detail.

Apart from the prescriptive texts in the Pentateuch, our other sources are the Psalter and, in a reflex kind of way, the prophets. The group of psalms individually headed 'Song of Ascents' (Pss. 120–34) appear to have formed a kind of hymnal for pilgrims to Jerusalem in much the same way as the 'Hallel' psalms came to have a part in certain of the festival celebrations. Strictly, only Psalm 122 has the explicit pilgrim theme, though the 'Songs of Ascents' taken as a whole have a disproportionately large number of mentions of Jerusalem and Zion in relation to the rest of the Psalter (21 per

---

[2] See, for example, K. van der Toorn, 'The Babylonian New Year Festival: New Insights from the Cuneiform Texts and their Bearing on Old Testament Study', *SVT* 43 (1991), 331–44. The use of the plural ('festivals') in the main text takes account of the fact that there were both spring and autumn Akitu ceremonies.

[3] We could also include here the imaginative reconstruction of a Danite autumn festival proposed by M. Goulder in *The Psalms of the Sons of Korah* (SJSOT 20; Sheffield: JSOT Press, 1982). See ch. 4.

cent). Psalm 122 expresses the pleasure of the pilgrim in having reached the holy citadel of Zion:

> I rejoiced with those who said to me,
> 'Let us go to the house of the Lord';
>
> Our feet are standing within your gates, O Jerusalem.
>
> (vv. 1–2)

These are the main pilgrim reminiscences in the psalm, though the reference to 'brothers and friends' in verse 8 may reflect the fellowship of pilgrimage that Josephus, in his paraphrase of the law on festivals, cites as one of the main purposes of pilgrimage.[4] Psalm 84 ('How lovely is your dwelling-place') also adverts to the pilgrim theme when praising those who have their hearts set on the pilgrim highways (v. 6[5]). Here the psalmist envisages the pilgrim caravans making their way through the Valley of Balsam Trees in the time of the former (i.e. autumn) rains (v. 7[6]), probably en route to the celebration of Tabernacles, the festival of the (autumnal) seventh month.

This is a meagre catch from the Psalter, but Psalm 48 – already the subject of chapter 4 – also sheds light on pilgrim worship at Zion.[5] As noted in chapter 4, some scholars have concluded that, since there is little in the historical books of the Old Testament to match the terms of Psalm 48, historical reminiscence plays little part in the psalm. However, this hardly does justice to certain features of the psalm, which refers to kings who came against Jerusalem and left in fear, and claims that a painful break in saving history has been healed as a result ('as we have heard, so have we seen', v. 9[8]). In celebration of all this, the psalmist calls for circumambulation of Zion and its towers, ramparts and citadels (vv. 13–14[12–13]). These are the ramparts and citadels for whose well-being Psalm 122 offers a prayer (v. 7). It is impossible to tell whether the circumambulation was formal and ceremonial or a purely private exercise, and we do not know what part such a celebration might have had in the annual $r^e galim$. On the basis of Psalm 132, one of the 'Songs of Ascents', and possibly such other psalms as 24 and 68, some have envisaged a role for the 'Ark of God' in the ceremonial when festival pilgrims went to Jerusalem to 'appear before God' (Exod. 23:17) or 'see the face of God' (Isa. 1:12).[6]

---

[4] *Ant.* 4:203; cf. Psalm 133:1.

[5] Cf. J.D. Levenson, *Sinai and Zion: An Entry into the Jewish Bible* (New Voices in Biblical Studies; Minneapolis: Winston Press, 1985), 146.

[6] See, however, 1 Kings 8:6.

The requirement that all adult males should make pilgrimage to the central sanctuary for the three major festivals was a considerable demand. In particular, the festival of Weeks came only seven weeks after Passover. Even the pious Tobit from Upper Galilee claims only to have gone 'often' to Jerusalem for the festivals (Tobit 1:6). The story of Elkanah's family, set in the pre-monarchical period, implies an *annual* visit to Shiloh, 'to offer the yearly sacrifice' (1 Sam. 1:21). Later, in the Second Temple period, it appears that even observant Jews satisfied themselves with an annual visit to Jerusalem.[7] By then the majority lived in the diaspora,[8] and the Old Testament laws did not extend to this situation. It was, in any case, impracticable to observe the *reḡalim* from such a distance. Even so, festivals meant large crowds converging upon Jerusalem, and this too affected the way in which the festivals were celebrated.[9]

Passover, which first appears as a family observance in Exodus 12, is presented as a communal celebration at the central sanctuary in Deuteronomy 16, according to which the Passover 'sacrifice' was to be slaughtered, cooked and eaten within the temple precincts (vv. 2, 7).[10] During the Second Temple period, however, the permitted area for eating was extended to include the whole city of Jerusalem, doubtless to accommodate the large numbers of pilgrims wishing to participate.[11] Now if such could happen in the historical period, it is not surprising to find the eschatologically oriented Zechariah 14 making similar provision for the end-time celebration of the festival of Tabernacles. The required attendance of the nations at this autumn celebration (vv. 16–19) would mean a flood of pilgrims coming into the city

---

[7] See S. Safrai, *Die Wallfahrt im Zeitalter des Zweiten Tempels* (Forschungen zum jüdisch-christlichen Dialog, 3; Neukirchen-Vluyn: Neukirchener Verlag, 1981), 38; idem, in S. Safrai and M. Stern (eds.), *The Jewish People in the First Century: Historical Geography, Political History, Social, Cultural and Religious Life and Institutions*, I (Compendia Rerum Iudaicarum ad Novum Testamentum, I; Assen: Van Gorcum, 1974), 191–204(191).

[8] Cf. Safrai, *Die Wallfahrt*, 6.

[9] For the suggestion that large-scale pilgrimage to Jerusalem was fostered by Herod the Great see M. Goodman, 'The Pilgrimage Economy of Jerusalem in the Second Temple Period', in L.I. Levine (ed.), *Jerusalem: Its Sanctity and Centrality to Judaism, Christianity, and Islam* (New York: Continuum, 1999), 69–76.

[10] There is no blood ritual in Deuteronomy 16, and the Passover 'sacrifice' can be from the 'flock or herd (*bāqār*)' (v. 2).

[11] Cf. m. Zeb. 5:8. See S. Safrai, 'Jerusalem in the Halacha of the Second Temple Period', in M. Poorthuis and Ch. Safrai (eds.), *The Centrality of Jerusalem: Historical Perspectives* (Kampen: Kok Pharos, 1996), 94–113(96, 101).

and the overstretching of the temple facilities. As we have noted in chapter 6, the mundane notice about cooking pots in verses 20–21 is meant to cater for the pilgrims, Jewish and Gentile, who would mass in Jerusalem for the worship of the Lord of hosts.[12]

If it was not customary to observe the full set of r*egalim*, we do not find the Israelite prophets berating the general population for laxity in festival attendance.[13] On the contrary, Amos taunts the north Israelites over their pilgrim trips to centres like Bethel, Gilgal and even the 'cross-border' Beersheba (Amos 4:4–5; 5:5; cf. Hos. 4:15). Nor is inattention to pilgrimage and festival observance cited among the reasons why Israel and Judah fell to the Mesopotamian superpowers in the eighth and sixth centuries respectively.[14] Rather, a typical prophetic perspective is expressed in the opening chapter of Isaiah where sacrifice, festival and the whole cultic apparatus are rejected because they reflect no inner spiritual reality on the part of those who throng Zion (Isa. 1:10–15).

We find, too, that it was not just adult males who attended the temple for the r*egalim*. The same Deuteronomy 16 that repeats the law on festivals (v. 16) also commands in connection with Weeks and Tabernacles that the pilgrims should celebrate at the central sanctuary with their sons and daughters, and their male and female slaves (vv. 11, 14). The practice in Elkanah's household has already been noted: the whole story of Hannah's initiative has for background the family's attendance at an annual Shilonite festival. So too, much later, Mary as well as Joseph, 'went to Jerusalem every year at the feast of the Passover' (Lk. 2:41). Women and pilgrimage form a natural pairing, as the history of Christian pilgrimage illustrates. Helena, the mother of Constantine, was the first in a long line of women pilgrims – Egeria, the two Melanias, Paula and Eudocia are other early names – who made pilgrimage to Palestine following Constantine's embracing of Christianity.

The Pilgrimage of the Nations

The Jerusalem pilgrimage theme takes a surprising turn when it is used to express the idea of an 'eschatological pilgrimage' of the

---

[12] And so no 'trader' would be required in the temple (v. 21); cf. S. Bergler, 'Jesus, Bar Kochba und das messianische Laubhüttenfest', *JSJ* 29 (1998), 143–91(151).

[13] It is noted in the historical books in connection with the celebration of Passover on a couple of occasions that the festival had not been celebrated on a comparable scale for many a day (2 Kgs. 23:22; 2 Chr. 30:26; 35:18) – whatever this may imply about normal observance.

[14] Cf. Safrai, *Die Wallfahrt*, 23.

nations to Zion to join in the worship of the God of Israel. Already
in the Second Temple period members of the Jewish diaspora commonly came to Jerusalem and stayed for shorter or longer periods –
some even dying there – so that they could study Torah with leading
authorities.[15] The Zion oracle in Isaiah 2 and Micah 4 visualizes the
nations coming to the specially elevated *Inselberg* of Zion to learn
the ways of God: 'for *torah* will go forth from Zion, and the word of
the Lord from Jerusalem' (Isa. 2:1–4[3]; Mic. 4:1–4[2]).[16] This idea
of the pilgrimage of the nations occurs elsewhere in the book of
Isaiah, at 56:6–8 and 66:18–24, and elsewhere in the prophets (cf.
Jer. 3:17; Zech. 8:20–23). Since Isaiah 1 is indeed introductory, in
the sense that it is concerned to present Isaiah's credentials as a
prophet no less than would a conventionally placed 'prophetic call
narrative',[17] the correspondence between 2:1–4 and 66:18–24
stands out more clearly, for it is as if the encompassing vision of the
book is that the Zion beloved of 'Isaiah of Jerusalem' is destined to
become the focus of universal pilgrimage.[18]

In Zechariah 14 this nation-pilgrimage is associated with the festival of Tabernacles (vv. 16–21). While there is no reference to Zion
as a specially elevated mountain in this section, the chapter talks of
the levelling of the area around Jerusalem and of the city remaining
aloft in its place (v. 10; cf. Isa. 2:1–4; Mic. 4:1–4).[19] As the last of the
festivals in the religious calendar, Tabernacles was regarded as the
appropriate occasion for the nations to express their submission to
the God of Israel. Nevertheless, the atmosphere in this excerpt from
the apocalyptically inclined book of Zechariah differs from that in
the Isaian-Mican oracle. No conversion of the nations is implied:[20]
they come to Jerusalem under compulsion (vv. 17–19). Moreover,
these end-time pilgrimages will be made by those who have survived
the destructive intervention of God at Jerusalem's last battle (cf.
Zeph. 3:8–10). Other texts reflect this more limited outlook, focus-
ing on the transference of the wealth of the nations to Israel, in

---

[15] Cf. Safrai in Safrai and Stern (eds.), *The Jewish People in the First Century*, I, 193–94.

[16] See the discussion in ch. 6.

[17] This is achieved by depicting Judah as having suffered the desolations against which Isaiah gave warning in oracles found in later chapters.

[18] Cf. A. Laato, *'About Zion I will not be Silent': The Book of Isaiah as an Ideological Unity* (CBOTS 44; Stockholm: Almqvist and Wiksell, 1998), 152.

[19] The point is noted in ch. 6.

[20] The contrast with Isaiah 56:6 is particularly strong in this respect (cf. Bergler, 'Jesus, Bar Kochba und das messianische Laubhüttenfest', 151–52).

token of their acknowledgement of Israel's God (Isa. 18:7; 60:5–7, 11, 13; 61:6; 66:12; Hag. 2:7; Ps. 68:29–31; Rev. 21:26).[21]

It has occasionally been suggested that the prophetic picture of Gentiles streaming to Jerusalem to bring their offerings to the God of Israel influenced Paul's attitude to his great project of conveying charitable aid from his Gentile converts to the impoverished Christian communities in Palestine. The large-scale incorporation of Gentiles into the Jewish church and the conviction that the 'last days' had been entered upon certainly provided the setting in which such an idea could have prospered. The apostle's thinking about this collection is expressed in his letters to two leading congregations (or groups of congregations) in Corinth and Rome. In 1 Corinthians 16:1–4 he answers an inquiry about the collection, while in 2 Corinthians he devotes two chapters to a commendation of the project (2 Cor. 8–9). The subject comes up again in his letter to the Roman church as he discusses his part in the dissemination of the gospel and his future plans in that regard (Rom. 15:23–33). The book of Acts also has relevant information. In Acts, Luke mentions a number of delegates from Gentile churches who accompanied Paul on his last journey to Jerusalem (Acts 20:4), and it is very probable that they had responsibility for the conveying of the collection to Jerusalem (cf. 1 Cor. 16:3–4). While Luke does not mention the handing over of the collection at the point where we should expect to hear of it (i.e. Acts 21:17–26), he has Paul announce later, in his defence before Felix, that part of the purpose of his Jerusalem visit was to convey charity to his nation (Acts 24:17).

Such is the basic outline of this first-century Christian project that has been linked with the Old Testament theme of the eschatological pilgrimage of the nations. For the connection to be established, correspondence could be sought at either or both of two levels: the collection itself could represent a first instalment of the Gentile wealth that was expected finally to flow into Jerusalem, or the arrival of the Gentile church delegates themselves could signal the beginning of the fulfilment of the Old Testament prophecies. This latter has been further explained as an ironic reversal of the Old Testament idea of Gentiles bringing Jews to the temple as an offering to the Lord (cf. Isa. 66:20). The Gentiles are then regarded as the 'true Israel' returning to Zion in

---

[21] Cf. Isaiah 45:14, in the context of the rise of Cyrus. There is a difference between pilgrimage texts and those that refer to return from exile, even though the distinction is not always easy to maintain (cf. Isa. 35:8–10; 51:11).

fulfilment of Old Testament prophecy,[22] and so Paul writes in Romans 15:16 of his 'priestly task to offer the Gentiles as an acceptable sacrifice' (cf. *REB*).

In his discussion of the collection Paul does not refer to the Old Testament pilgrimage texts. However, he introduces the collection in Romans 15 on the back of some reflections on his own part in the Gentile mission (Rom. 15:23–33, following 15:14–22), and the collection is seen as an episode in that programme.[23] Luke, by contrast, is strikingly reticent about the whole undertaking. He does not tell us that the delegates listed in Acts 20:4 were assisting with the collection; and when Paul and his colleagues reached Jerusalem he records only that the party and their report of Gentile conversions were received warmly (Acts 21:17–20). As we have seen, it is only in Paul's account of himself before Felix that the purpose of the visit to Jerusalem is explained (Acts 24:17). Luke may well have had his own reasons for playing down the significance of the collection.[24] Perhaps it was sufficient for him that Paul was arrested and eventually forwarded to Rome for trial as a direct result of his conversations with the Jerusalem church leaders after the collection had been delivered to them (see Acts 21:20–30).

On balance, it seems unlikely that the fulfilment of Old Testament prophecy played more than a very minor part in Paul's thinking about the collection. Far from suggesting a triumphant arrival in Jerusalem with the tokens of Gentile submission, his first mention of the subject leaves in doubt his own participation in the actual journey (1 Cor. 16:4). When he returns to the subject in Romans 15 he is apprehensive about the attitude of the Jerusalem Christians to the fruit of his efforts (vv. 30–32). Moreover, he has plans for extensive travel post-Jerusalem (Rom. 15:23–44, 28): the eschaton is not yet! His motivation in promoting the collection by the Gentile churches is indicated as first charitable, then as reciprocation for spiritual benefits received from the mother churches in Judea, and thirdly as a sign of God's grace in what were formerly fallow fields (cf. Rom. 15:26–27; 2 Cor. 8:1–5, 13–15; 9:13–15). There is, too, the general question of the place of Jerusalem in Paul's writings,

---

[22] Cf. K.F. Nickle, *The Collection: A Study in Paul's Strategy* (Studies in Biblical Theology, 48; London: SCM Press, 1966), 139; F.F. Bruce, 'Paul and Jerusalem', *Tyndale Bulletin* 19 (1968), 3–25(23–24); E.P. Sanders, *Paul, the Law, and the Jewish People* (Philadelphia: Fortress/London:SCM, 1983/1985), 171–73, 199–200; idem, 'Jerusalem and its Temple in Early Christian Thought and Practice', in Levine (ed.), *Jerusalem*, 90–103(97–100, 102).

[23] Cf. Bruce, 'Paul and Jerusalem', 23.

[24] Nickle, *The Collection*, 149–50, thinks that Paul's carrying of funds to the Jerusalem church could have been deemed illegal by the Roman authorities.

where it is scarce mentioned. His one considered reference in the context of the new Christian order (see Gal. 4:21–31) does not suggest that it had such a positive symbolical importance as the 'Pauline pilgrimage' theory would require. It is a small step from Galatians 4 to what is effectively the spiritualizing of the Jerusalem pilgrimage theme by the writer of Hebrews, according to whom the Christian believer has come, not to a physical Mount Sinai, but 'to Mount Zion and to the city of the living God, the heavenly Jerusalem …' (Heb. 12:22). Realized eschatology of this sort left little room for such a synthetic anticipation of the eschaton as has been suggested for the collection on behalf of the Palestinian poor.

Jewish Pilgrim Piety after the Second Destruction

The biblical laws of pilgrimage could no longer be applied after the Roman destruction of the temple. Visits to Jerusalem became more a matter of personal piety. Following the second Jewish-Roman war of AD 132–135 the emperor Hadrian issued a decree banishing Jews from their holy city, which he now renamed Aelia Capitolina. Thereafter the centre of gravity for Palestinian Judaism shifted to Galilee, and to Tiberias in particular.[25] In a well-known passage in his commentary on Zephaniah, Jerome mentions the Hadrianic interdict and the special concession on the Ninth of Ab allowing Jews to congregate in Jerusalem to mourn the destruction of their temple.[26] His description of those who met to mourn exudes little sympathy: *decrepitas mulierculas, et senes pannis annisque obsitos, in corporibus et in habitu suo iram Domini demonstrantes* ('decrepit women, and old men burdened with rags and years, demonstrating in their bodies and in their garments the wrath of the Lord'). This was a scene witnessed already in AD 333 by the Bordeaux Pilgrim and noted in his itinerary.[27] However, the effects of the Hadrianic interdict appear not to have been so comprehensive

---

[25] Cf. M. Friedman, 'Jewish Pilgrimage after the Destruction of the Second Temple', in N. Rosovsky (ed.), *City of the Great King: Jerusalem from David to the Present* (Cambridge, MA: Harvard University Press, 1996), 136–46(137).

[26] *Comm. in Soph.* 1, 15–16 (CCSL 76A [1970]), 673–74. See R.L. Wilken, 'Christian Pilgrimage to the Holy Land', in Rosovsky (ed.), *City of the Great King*, 117–35(121–22).

[27] *Itinerarium Burdigalense* 591 (CCSL 175 [1965], 16); cf. J. Wilkinson, 'Christian Pilgrims in Jerusalem during the Byzantine Period', *PEQ* 108 (1976), 75–101(81); G. Bowman, '"Mapping History's Redemption": Eschatology and Topography in the *Itinerarium Burdigalense*', in Levine (ed.), *Jerusalem*, 163–87.

or so drastic as they have sometimes been represented. During the Roman period Jews still managed to make pilgrimages throughout the year to Jerusalem,[28] and a group of disciples of R. Meir may even have been able to settle in Jerusalem at the end of the second century.[29]

The visiting of the tombs of the righteous, already a feature of Second Temple Jewish piety, also continued. The practice was early adopted by Christian pilgrims, as we shall see. In time, the traditional Jewish understanding of uncleanness as conveyed by contact with corpses was revised so that the remains of the righteous were deemed not to be subject to corruption (cf. Ps. 16:10, 'You will not abandon me to Sheol, nor will you let your holy one see corruption'). Places of burial could therefore be entered without fear of contracting uncleanness.[30] It was a timely development in view of the 'tactile piety' that, in the same period, made *Christians* eager to touch the very bones and relics of the martyrs and saints.[31]

At an early stage the mourning of those who came to see the ruined temple became ritualized, with even the rending of garments being regulated.[32] On the other hand, fragments from the Cairo Genizah, representing the Islamic period, attest not only to mourning ritual but also to the persistent expectation that God would again restore the ruins of Zion. Those who made pilgrimage were bidden: 'circumambulate all the gates and all the corners, go round Zion and encircle her, count her towers' – in obvious recollection of Psalm 48 and the worship of pre-exilic times.[33]

---

[28] Cf. Safrai in Safrai and Stern (eds.), *The Jewish People in the First Century*, I, 211; Friedman, 'Jewish Pilgrimage', 137.

[29] S. Safrai, 'The Holy Congregation of Jerusalem', *ScrHieros* 23 (1972), 62–78(77).

[30] See J. Wilkinson, 'Visits to Jewish Tombs by Early Christians', in *Akten des XII. Internationalen Kongresses für christliche Archäologie*, I (Jahrbuch für Antike und Christentum Ergänzungsband, 20, 1; Münster: Aschendorffsche Verlagsbuchhandlung, 1995), 452–65(463).

[31] See Wilken, 'Christian Pilgrimage', 131.

[32] See b. MQ 26a.

[33] The relevant fragment is listed as Ms Adler 2893 at the Jewish Theological Seminary of America in New York. For the text see M. Margalioth, *Halakhoth on the Land of Israel from the Genizah* (Heb.) (Jerusalem: Mossad Harav Kook, 1973), 139–41(141). See further S.C. Reif, 'Some Recent Developments in the Study of Medieval Hebrew Liturgy', in N.R.M. de Lange (ed.), *Hebrew Scholarship and the Mediaeval World* (Cambridge: Cambridge University Press, 2001), 60–73(69–71).

Pilgrimage in the Early Christian Centuries

Christian pilgrimage before Constantine is not well documented, and it is disputed whether the known cases qualify as 'pilgrimage'.[34] The main visits of which we know were by church dignitaries such as Melito, bishop of Sardis, and Origen; and they went to Palestine to visit biblical sites and to confirm for themselves the authenticity of the biblical tradition.[35] The objective was not pilgrimage in the ordinary sense: a form of *historia* was being undertaken.[36] In the New Testament the verb *historein* is used by Paul of the occasion when he 'went up' to Jerusalem to meet Peter (Gal. 1:18). The word attracts translations like 'get to know' (*REB*) and 'visit' (*NRSV*), in keeping with Hellenistic rather than classical usage. In the context, Paul is explaining how he came to his understanding of the Christian gospel, claiming that it came by divine revelation rather than by consulting with human authorities (vv. 11–17). He then notes that 'after three years' he went up to Jerusalem and saw Peter and James (vv. 18–19). The question is whether the use of the verb *historein* implies more than getting to know the leaders and, if so, whether this is compatible with the argument in the preceding verses. The case is finely balanced. The use of *historein* by Paul, if he were intending to avoid the idea of consultation in Jerusalem – the kind of consultation that he describes for a later visit (cf. Gal. 2:1–2) – would be a little surprising. It would have been remarkable, too, if during a fortnight's visit to Jerusalem he avoided discussion of the eyewitness testimony of the leading apostles.[37] It is possible, then, to

---

[34] See J. Engemann, 'Das Jerusalem der Pilger, Kreuzauffindung und Wallfahrt', in *Akten des XII. Internationalen Kongresses für christliche Archäologie*, I (Jahrbuch für Antike und Christentum Ergänzungsband, 20, 1; Münster: Aschendorffsche Verlagsbuchhandlung, 1995), 24–35(26); J. Wilkinson, 'Jewish Holy Places and the Origins of Christian Pilgrimage', in R. Ousterhout (ed.), *The Blessings of Pilgrimage* (Illinois Byzantine Studies, 1; Urbana: University of Illinois Press, 1990), 41–53(44); idem, 'Visits to Jewish Tombs', 452–65(464); K.G. Holum, 'Hadrian and St. Helena: Imperial Travel and the Origins of Christian Holy Land Pilgrimage', in Ousterhout (ed.), *The Blessings,* 66–81(68–70); Wilken, 'Christian Pilgrimage', 124–25.

[35] See Wilkinson, 'Jewish Holy Places', 44, 52.

[36] Cf. Joan E. Taylor, *Christians and the Holy Places: The Myth of Jewish-Christian Origins* (Oxford: Clarendon, 1993), 310–11; E.D. Hunt, *Holy Land Pilgrimage in the Later Roman Empire AD 312–460* (Oxford: Clarendon, 1982), 77–78, 94.

[37] Such an assumption is very easily and naturally made, as can be illustrated from the devotional study by J. Stuart Holden, *The Master and His*

see Paul himself as the first in the succession of Christian 'pilgrim inquirers' to visit Jerusalem, even if people rather than places were his chief interest.[38]

Visitors to Jerusalem between AD 70 and Constantine were confronted by the abject ruins of the temple, whatever else attracted their attention.[39] The Christian pilgrim experience changed profoundly in the fourth century, however, with the building of the Constantinian basilicas. It is unlikely that Constantine himself ever got as far as Palestine in his travels.[40] Instead, he sent Helena his mother, who 'progressed' through the region in the manner of a Tudor monarch, bestowing favours and initiating royal projects. More classically, her tour has been compared with the imperial *itinera principum*,[41] though it has been claimed that she was simply being 'used' by her son to consolidate his hold on this corner of the empire.[42] As a result of her 'progress', the basilicas at Bethlehem and Olivet were built,[43] Palestine gained recognition as 'Holy Land' for Christians as well as for Jews,[44] and Christian shrines were

---

[37] (*continued*) *Men* ([repr.] Belfast: Ambassador Publications, 2002), 102–103: 'It is not difficult to imagine Peter showing his guest ... round the places which had become sacred from their association with Jesus, until the Temple Courts, and the way out to Bethany, and Solomon's Porch and its sheep-pool, and the Upper Room, and the Garden ... were as familiar to Paul as to Peter himself. Is it difficult to imagine the thousand and one questions Paul put ...?' While this piece of imaginative writing focuses more on places than on issues, and does not take into account Paul's own acquaintance with Jerusalem (cf. Acts 22:3; 26:4), its approach is more convincing than those depictions of Paul which turn him into some kind of first-century Rudolf Bultmann; even in Athens Paul went about with his eyes open (Acts 17:23). The book by Holden was kindly sent to me by Mr Thomas Pinkerton, of Faith House, Belfast.

[38] See the discussion by W.D. Davies, *The Setting of the Sermon on the Mount* (Brown Judaic Studies, 186; Atlanta: Scholars Press, 1989), 453–55.

[39] See Taylor, *Christians and the Holy Places*, 313, on pre-Constantinian visitors coming to see the land laid low, those thereafter to see it in its glory.

[40] Cf. Hunt, *Holy Land Pilgrimage*, 6.

[41] See Holum, 'Hadrian and St. Helena', 72–77.

[42] So Taylor, *Christians and the Holy Places*, 307–308.

[43] But Eusebius, the principal source, does not associate Helena with the building in the area of Golgotha (cf. Hunt, *Holy Land Pilgrimage*, 37–38).

[44] See Dorothea R. French, 'Journeys to the Center of the Earth: Medieval and Renaissance Pilgrimages to Mount Calvary', in Barbara N. Sargent-Baur (ed.), *Journeys Toward God: Pilgrimage and Crusade* (Occasional Studies Series, 5; Kalamazoo, MI: SMC XXX Medieval Institute

established as alternative foci to the pagan versions already spread throughout the empire.[45]

From then on, pilgrims and pilgrimages proliferated. Holy sites were identified and the identifications were usually accepted gratefully by the pious traveller. Egeria, whose travels also took her to Sinai and into Mesopotamia, was typical in being disposed to believe almost anything that she was told.[46] Pilgrims were shown such improbable antiques as Elijah's bed in Sarepta[47] and, if they travelled to Arabia, Job's dunghill.[48] At Nazareth the Jewish community even organized the famous bench miracle for credulous Christian pilgrims. Visitors to Nazareth, reported the pilgrim of Piacenza, were shown the book in which Christ practised his alphabet and the bench on which he used to sit with other children. Local Jews affected not to be able to move the bench, though Christians, as if by a miracle, moved it about without difficulty.[49]

With the construction of the basilicas at Bethlehem and Golgotha, and on the Mount of Olives, 'stational liturgy' – the commemorating *in situ* of the events of Christ's life, death, resurrection and ascension – began to develop.[50] The Holy Week liturgy could now follow the last days and hours at the actual locations where the saving events took place. However, the earliest Christian visitors to Palestine had shown as much interest in Old Testament tombs as in Christian ones,[51] and this continued even after Constantine's

---

[44] (*continued*) Publications, Western Michigan University, 1992), 45–81(48). At the same time, there were many survivals of the pre-Constantinian period, even in Jerusalem. Even the name Aelia remained as an official designation in Byzantine texts – a usage to which Eusebius happily subscribed (cf. Hunt, *Holy Land Pilgrimage*, 149).

[45] Cf. Taylor, *Christians and the Holy Places*, 308–309.

[46] See Hunt, *Holy Land Pilgrimage*, 87–88.

[47] The Piacenza Pilgrim, *Travels*, 2; text in Eng. tr. in J. Wilkinson, *Jerusalem Pilgrims Before the Crusades* (Warminster: Aris and Phillips, 1977), 79.

[48] See Wilken, 'Christian Pilgrimage', 127, 497n. 31.

[49] The Piacenza Pilgrim, *Travels*, 5; text in Eng. tr. in Wilkinson, *Jerusalem Pilgrims*, 79. See also Taylor, *Christians and the Holy Places*, 328.

[50] Cf. Wilken, 'Christian Pilgrimage', 130; Wendy Pullan, 'Mapping Time and Salvation: Early Christian Pilgrimage to Jerusalem', in G.D. Flood (ed.), *Mapping Invisible Worlds* (Cosmos 9; Edinburgh: Edinburgh University Press, 1993), 34. Wilkinson, *Jerusalem Pilgrims*, 35, compares the sequence of saving events represented by the three 'holy caves' at Bethlehem, Golgotha and Olivet with the Christological sections of the third-century Baptismal Creed and the *Te Deum*; cf. idem, 'Christian Pilgrims', 97.

[51] On Christian interest in Jewish tombs see Wilkinson, 'Visits to Jewish Tombs', 452–65.

building projects.[52] Visits to the 'Tombs of the Patriarchs' at Hebron continued: we even hear of parallel Jewish and Christian ceremonies being carried out there.[53] Evidence of Christian attendance at *Christian* tombs comes from as early as the mid- to late-second century, in the *Martyrium Polycarpi*, in which the friends of the Smyrnan martyr speak of their intention of holding annual commemorations at his tomb.[54]

The popularization of pilgrimage upon Constantine's conversion was welcomed with reserve by the theologians of the fourth century. Cyril of Jerusalem was an enthusiast and an exception. Cyril had a fairly developed sense of what the deceased apostles, prophets and martyrs could achieve on behalf of the church militant, and pilgrimage fitted well in that view of things.[55] Others tried to stem the flow of pilgrims to Zion. Eusebius of Caesarea, the compiler of a gazetteer of biblical sites, did not encourage pilgrim preoccupation with them.[56] Most cited of all in this regard is Gregory of Nyssa, whose own visit to Palestine in the line of duty convinced him that every kind of rascality prospered in Jerusalem. Cappadocia had sites more holy than those of the holy land itself.[57] Athanasius of Alexandria shows himself a model of pastoral insight and sensitivity in his 'Letter to Virgins who went to Pray in Jerusalem and Returned', originally written in Greek but surviving in a Syriac translation dating to the sixth or seventh century.[58] The

---

[52] Cf. Wilkinson, 'Jewish Holy Places', 44–45.

[53] See The Piacenza Pilgrim, *Travels*, 30; text in Eng. tr. in Wilkinson, *Jerusalem Pilgrims*, 85.

[54] *Letter of the Smyrnaeans* 18 (ed. J.B. Lightfoot, *The Apostolic Fathers* [2nd edn], II, 3 [London: Macmillan, 1889], 396-97 [Greek], 484–85 [English]).

[55] *Mystagogical Lecture* 5:9 (Eng. tr. in L.P. McCauley and A.A. Stephenson [eds.], *The Works of Saint Cyril of Jerusalem*, 2 [Washington: Catholic University of America Press, 1970], 197); cf. Wilkinson, 'Visits to Jewish Tombs', 457.

[56] Cf. P.W.L. Walker, *Holy City, Holy Places? Christian Attitudes to Jerusalem and the Holy Land in the Fourth Century* (Oxford: Clarendon, 1990), 104–106. Some qualification of Walker's position is suggested by R.L. Wilken, *The Land Called Holy: Palestine in Christian History and Thought* (New Haven: Yale University Press, 1992), 291n. 27.

[57] 'On Pilgrimages', Eng. tr. in H. Wace and P. Schaff (eds.), *Gregory of Nyssa* (Nicene and Post-Nicene Fathers of the Christian Church [Second Series], 5; Oxford: Parker and Co./New York: Christian Literature Company, 1893), 383; cf. Hunt, *Holy Land Pilgrimage*, 91.

[58] Syriac text and French translation in J. Lebon, 'Athanasiana Syriaca II: Une Lettre Attribuée à Saint Athanase d'Alexandrie', *Le Muséon* 41 (1928), 169–216. See also Susanna Elm, 'Perceptions of Jerusalem

addressees had visited the holy places in Palestine and were now lamenting their distance from them. Athanasius reminds them that Christ's presence cannot be limited to any particular spot, and he commends to them the examples of such as Peter, Zacchaeus and Mary of Bethany who disentangled themselves from worldly interests in order to be attached to Christ.[59] The addressees, if they hold fast to Christ, will be found not to have journeyed far from the holy places.[60]

Retrospect

For their own reasons, pilgrims both Jewish and Christian have made a priority of pilgrimaging to Jerusalem-Zion.[61] There were other foci of attention in antiquity, but Zion was for the time being 'the highest of the mountains' (cf. Isa. 2:2). Even Sinai, the mountain of the law-giving, appears never to have excited pilgrim interest in a comparable fashion,[62] though Martin Noth thought to have discovered evidence of pilgrim interest behind the wilderness itinerary in Numbers 33.[63] When the prophet Elijah hurried there for protection from Queen Jezebel, it was only to hear the divine voice inquiring what he was doing there (1 Kgs. 19:9, 13). Rather, the Old Testament even manages to subsume Sinai under Zion. In the end-time, not only will the law be dispensed from Zion (Isa. 2:3//Mic. 4:2), but the cloud and fire of Sinai and of the wilderness 'pilgrimage' that followed are envisaged as settling over

---

[58] (*continued*) Pilgrimage as Reflected in Two Early Sources on Female Pilgrimage (3rd and 4th Centuries A.D.)', *Studia Patristica* 20 (1989), 219–23(219–21); Georgia A. Frank, 'Pilgrim's Experience and Theological Challenge: Two Patristic Views', in *Akten des XII. Internationalen Kongresses für christliche Archäologie*, II (Jahrbuch für Antike und Christentum Ergänzungsband, 20, 2; Münster: Aschendorffsche Verlagsbuchhandlung, 1995), 787–91.

[59] Fol. 105a–b (Syriac text, Lebon, 173–74 [French tr., 191–92]).

[60] Fol. 103d (Syriac text, Lebon, 172 [French tr., 190]): 'Take courage, then, and do not grieve; you are not far removed from the holy places. For where Christ dwells, there is holiness, and where there is the presence of Christ, there also are the riches of holy joy.'

[61] Cf. Hunt, *Holy Land Pilgrimage*, 84, on the unimportance of Rome for the Bordeaux Pilgrim: '*Urbs Roma* was, for the pilgrim, only a stage on the return journey – nothing of its great past seems to have stirred his enthusiasm.'

[62] Sinai was, of course, less accessible than Zion for the average Israelite.

[63] M. Noth, 'Der Wallfahrtsweg zum Sinai (4. Mose 33)', *Palästinajahrbuch* 36 (1940), 5–28(8).

Mount Zion (Isa. 4:5).[64] It is the equivalent of bringing the caravan into the drawing room.

Yet in other texts, and without reference to pilgrimage, the generations of the Old Testament, far from being cut off from the Sinai of the remote past, are associated idealistically (or 'mystically') with it in a way that bridges the years between the original event and each individual generation. This is the significance of Deuteronomy 5:3: 'Not with our fathers did the Lord make this covenant, but with us, who are all of us here alive today.'[65] But, of course, the assumption of the Pentateuchal narrative is that the generation of the Plain of Moab was not the generation that had been the contracting party at Sinai (cf. Deut. 1:34–39). What is meant in Deuteronomy 5 is that the Sinaitic covenant is renewed for each succeeding generation of Israelites. In later times, and with similar intent, the Passover haggadah would instruct each Israelite to consider himself as having come up out of Egypt.[66] By a comparable reckoning, the theology of Christian baptism expounded in Romans 6 unites the individual Christian believer to the original event in the dying and rising of Christ (vv. 1–14). Each of these insights operates on a different plane from the 'ritualized re-enactment of biblical events' that is characteristic of early Christian (and Jewish) pilgrimage.[67] They do not depend upon physical presence at a particular site.

On the strictest definition, pilgrimage takes in the journey as much as the goal of the journey. R.W. Frank introduces the very striking figure of pilgrims travelling to and from their destination 'in a kind of "force field"' of religious preoccupation.[68] This seems particularly appropriate when the pilgrimage involves visits to multiple sites, as commonly for Holy Land pilgrims. Such journeying could indeed be a deeply religious experience, as it was for the like of Egeria and Paula. It may therefore be appropriate that Jerome's account of Paula's travels about Palestine exhibits something of his commentary method,[69] with its cross-references to biblical texts and allegorizing of place names

---

[64] See further J.P. Schultz, 'From Sacred Space to Sacred Object to Sacred Person in Jewish Antiquity', *Shofar* 12 (1993), 28–37(31).

[65] Other texts that move in the same orbit include Deuteronomy 4:10–15; 29:14–15.

[66] See m. Pes. 10:5 ('In every generation a man ought to regard himself as if he came out of Egypt').

[67] Cf. G. Vikan, 'Pilgrims in Magi's Clothing: The Impact of Mimesis on Early Byzantine Pilgrimage Art', in Ousterhout (ed.), *The Blessings of Pilgrimage*, 97–107(99).

[68] R.W. Frank, 'Pilgrimage and Sacral Power', in Sargent-Baur (ed.), *Journeys Towards God*, 31–43(33).

[69] Cf. Wilkinson, *Jerusalem Pilgrims*, 2.

producing a slightly 'Bunyanesque' effect. Doubtless much of this is Jerome's own gloss on Paula's travels, but, since he was her mentor and fellow pilgrim, at least some of the explanations and associations that feature in the account could have been shared during the actual pilgrimage nineteen years previously. Even so, did she really decide not to visit Kiriath-Sepher because it could be translated 'City of the Book' and therefore fell on the wrong side of the Pauline divide between 'the letter that kills' and 'the Spirit that gives life'?[70] Other pilgrims experienced a different reality, not being able to insulate themselves from other, more earthly minded, travellers on the roads, or avoid the dangers of the hostelries at night. Such things threatened to compromise Christian discipline, and were a further reason why Gregory of Nyssa remained sceptical about the value of pilgrimage.[71]

Nevertheless, the journey was important, and already our Old Testament texts illustrate how it could be suffused with religious purpose and expectation (cf. Ps. 84:6[5]; 'Songs of Ascents'). In this respect, Zechariah 14 makes contribution in its peculiar way, when it says that the bells on the horses participating in the end-time pilgrimages will bear the legend 'Holy to the Lord'. This is the inscription that appears on the turban of the Israelite high priest (see Exod. 28:36–37), and its occurrence in Zechariah 14:20 is therefore surprising. At the least, it seems to be implied that the journey to Zion by the pilgrimaging nations will share the sacred status of the festival that draws them there.

Pilgrimage then, as now, was concerned to a very considerable degree with sites associated with special people and events from the past – places where it was reckoned that spiritual benefit might still be experienced. Zechariah 14 reminds us, however, that there was sometimes a future dimension to pilgrimage. For both Jews and Christians Palestine was the land where God would act in the future, and Jerusalem stood centre stage. For both, a visit to the Mount of Olives could conjure up scenes of divine intervention on a future day, whether on the basis of Zechariah 14:4 ('On that day his feet will stand on the Mount of Olives')[72] or of Acts 1:11 ('This

---

[70] Cf. 2 Corinthians 3:6.

[71] Cf. Hunt, *Holy Land Pilgrimage*, 69–75. For the frustrations of the modern pilgrim competing with less exalted, touristic, interests see D. Klatzker, 'Sacred Journeys: Jerusalem in the Eyes of American Travelers before 1948', in Y. Ben-Arieh and M. Davis (eds.), *Jerusalem in the Mind of the Western World, 1800–1948* (With Eyes Toward Zion, 5; Westport: Praeger, 1997), 47–58(51–52).

[72] The frescoes from the Dura-Europos synagogue in Babylonia, dating to not later than the early third century AD, include a resurrection scene largely based on Zechariah 14 and involving the Mount of Olives. See

same Jesus ... will come back in the same way as you have seen him go into heaven'). On the Christian side, even the horse-bells (or adornments) of Zechariah 14:20 come into play in the fourth century and onwards. On 25 February in AD 395 Ambrose bishop of Milan preached his funeral eulogy *De Obitu Theodosii*, in which he referred to the tradition that Helena sent the nails of the Crucifixion to Constantine, one for his diadem and one to form part of a bridle for the emperor's horse.[73] In this way, Zechariah 14:20 was fulfilled: the bridle was *sanctum domino*, 'holy to the Lord', and Constantine's submission to Christ had inaugurated the 'day' of Zechariah 14:20. Jerome ridiculed this unlikely fulfilment of the biblical text, but the idea persisted.[74]

---

[72] (*continued*) H. Riesenfeld, *The Resurrection in Ezekiel xxxvii and in the Dura-Europos Paintings* (Uppsala Universitets Årsskrift, 11; Uppsala: Almqvist and Wiksell, 1948), 28–34 (this study is reprinted in J. Gutman [ed.], *No Graven Images: Studies in Art and the Hebrew Bible* [New York: Ktav, 1971]).

[73] *De Obitu Theodosii* 47 (*PL* 16, cols. 1401–2). The word usually translated 'bells' in Zechariah 14:20 is a *hapax legomenon* and was rendered 'bridles' by the major ancient versions (cf. also *A*Vmg).

[74] See Hunt, *Holy Land Pilgrimage*, 41–42. The anonymous *Life of Constantine*, 4 mentions that Helena sent nails to Constantine; see text in Eng. tr. in Wilkinson, *Jerusalem Pilgrims*, 202.

Chapter Eight

Literalism, Determinism and the Future

In earlier chapters we have been dealing in hyperbole and vision, and in Israelite-Jewish aspirations for the 'ultimate future' of a people that had long experienced the heavy hand of history. In the short concluding chapter we shall be reminded of Christ's words about the worship that God seeks – 'neither on this mountain, nor in Jerusalem' (Jn 4:21) – a worship that is already inaugurated in the response of those who worship the Father in spirit and in truth (v. 23). The problems come when, in seeking to flesh out the biblical prospectus, we attempt to transpose the (mainly) Old Testament images and prophecies into contemporary or future geopolitical realities.

The Nineteenth Century

For many Jews and Christians the proclamation of the modern state of Israel in 1948 has created the context in which the ancient biblical prophecies can be activated, and in a generally literal kind of way. To date, this 'restoration' of Israel has brought relief and prosperity to many of its citizens, but the journey has been problem laden and tragedy prone. Even so, many Zionists, both Jewish and Christian, hold that the creation of the state of Israel is in accordance with God's purposes and in fulfilment of biblical prophecy.

So the precarious perching of modern Israel among its Arab neighbours relates very directly to the 'land theology' of the Old Testament, developed between two and three thousand years previously. The wider world sees this as a Jewish issue, but it is also a Christian one, and in at least two respects. It is an issue for Christians insofar as it is incumbent on them as readers of both Testaments to make sense of the land dimension in the Old Testament's envisioning of Israel's future. It is also a Christian problem in the sense that Christian interpretation of biblical texts, and the will to bring about the fulfilment of those texts as interpreted, has contributed significantly to the emergence of modern Israel.

As is well known, the notion that Palestine was largely unpopulated in the nineteenth century helped spring the modern Zionist cause into action. It was a view that was widespread in Europe, and it was not limited to Jewish Zionist circles. In the early nineteenth century interested Christian parties in England and Prussia were already pressing for the 'return' of Jews to Palestine, and suggesting that a relatively unoccupied land was waiting to receive them.[1] The idea was popularized in the familiar coinage, 'A land without a people for a people without a land', and it was firmly believed by Christians as prominent and as influential as the seventh Earl of Shaftesbury, whose diary entry for 17 May 1854 notes: 'Syria "is wasted without an inhabitant" ... There is a country *without a nation*; and God now, in His wisdom and mercy, directs us to *a nation without a country*. His own once loved, nay, still loved people, the sons of Abraham, of Isaac, and of Jacob.'[2] James Finn, the British Consul in Jerusalem, wrote to Lord Clarendon at the Foreign Office in 1857, saying that the country

> is in a considerable degree empty of inhabitants and therefore its greatest need is that of a body of population ... It is therefore important for the Sultan to procure a population which should be grateful and loyal – and to take the initiative in putting them into the country ... Such a people may be found in the Jews: for their affections are centred here: and they own no willing subjection to any European crown.[3]

Whatever the truth in these claims mid-century, they were challenged by Ahad Ha\u1d9cam from as early as 1891, when he observed that there was then very little uncultivated land anywhere in the country.[4]

---

[1] Cf. K. Crombie, *For the Love of Zion: Christian Witness and the Restoration of Israel* (London: Hodder and Stoughton, 1991), 4–5.

[2] See E. Hodder, *The Life and Work of the Seventh Earl of Shaftesbury, K.G.* (popular edn; London: Cassell, 1888), 493.

[3] See A.M. Hyamson (ed.), *The British Consulate in Jerusalem in Relation to the Jews of Palestine 1838–1914*, I (Publications of the Jewish Historical Society of England; London: Edward Goldston, 1939), 249–50. The quotations are taken from Finn's seven 'propositions' in connection with the transplantation of Jewish people to Palestine. In his accompanying commentary he shows that he had a particular kind of 'Jew' in mind: 'I reply, that it is not necessary to regard all the Hebrew nation as anti-Christian. I have seen it asserted by a good authority that there are now to be found in Europe and America, a sufficient number of baptized Christian Israelites, if they could be assembled together, to give a tolerable population to Palestine' (Hyamson, 251). Cf. Crombie, *For the Love of Zion*, 93.

[4] 'From 1891 on Ahad Ha-'Am stressed that Palestine was not only a small land but not an empty one ... He pointed out that there was little untilled soil in Palestine, except for stony hills or sand dunes' (H. Kohn, quoted in M. Menuhin, *The Decadence of Judaism in our Time* [Beirut: The Institute

If there had been any element of misrepresentation in what Ahad HaCam was rejecting, distance and ignorance will have played a part. At the same time, revisionism, however it came about, would have been a convenient ally of the ideology of 'return'. The notion of the uninhabited land is not unknown in previous tellings of Israel's story. Hecataeus of Abdera claimed that the Jews, on being expelled from Egypt, entered Judea, which at the time was quite unpopulated.[5] Modern responses to the challenges of the Middle East have the additional hazard of the 'self-fulfilling prophecy' to negotiate. As the seventh Earl of Shaftesbury discovered, it was possible to force the hand of history, and by so doing to forfeit one's confidence in God's involvement in the resultant developments.[6]

---

[4] (*continued*) for Palestine Studies, 1965(1969)], 63. The original article appeared in *Menorah Journal* [Autumn-Winter Issue, 1958], but was unavailable to me.) Theodor Herzl, the inspiration behind the modern Zionist enterprise, had considered the 'problem' of the Arab inhabitants of Palestine and noted in his diary entry for 12 June 1895 that the 'penniless population' would need to be spirited across the border to make way for the incoming Zionists. See G.M. Burge, *Whose Land? Whose Promise? What Christians Are Not Being Told about Israel and the Palestinians* (Carlisle: Paternoster Press, 2003), 136.

[5] See D. Mendels, 'Hecataeus of Abdera and a Jewish "patrios politeia" of the Persian Period (Diodorus Siculus XL,3)', *ZAW* 95 (1983), 96–110(98). Mendels suggests a similar presentation of Jerusalem, after the Babylonian exile, in Nehemiah 2–4, and also compares the depiction of the land as a whole in Judith 5:19 (cf. v. 18) (99). M. Weinfeld, *The Promise of the Land: The Inheritance of the Land of Canaan by the Israelites* (The Taubman Lectures in Jewish Studies, 3; Berkeley: University of California Press, 1993), 209–13, discusses the whole issue of the transformation of the idea of conquest of the land into willing evacuation, or prior Israelite possession and Canaanite invasion, or accommodation to Canaanites if they repented.

[6] Witness his anguished entry in his diary for 15 December 1845, following the report of the death of Michael Alexander, the first Anglican bishop in Jerusalem: 'But what is our condition? Have we run counter to the will of God? Have we conceived a merely human project, and then imagined it to be a decree of the Almighty, when we erected a bishopric in Jerusalem, and appointed a Hebrew to exercise the functions? Have we vainly and presumptuously attempted to define "the times and seasons which the Father hath put in His own power"?' (see Hodder, *The Life and Work*, 329). That Shaftesbury should entertain such radical doubt simply in response to Alexander's death after an episcopate of four years may surprise; this may, however, be as much an indication of how closely he linked the establishing of the Jerusalem episcopate with the last phases of the prophetic programme that he thought to have found in Scripture. For a short account of Alexander's appointment and exercise of his bishopric see Crombie, *For the Love of Zion*, 36–69.

The developing Christian interest in the land of Israel during the nineteenth century was the product of several different impulses: the rise of evangelicalism following the Evangelical Awakening, growing interest in mission, including missions to Jews, interest in Bible study and in biblical prophecy, eschatological expectation in the context of the French Revolution[7] and the Napoleonic wars, the rise of romanticism and orientalism, and the broadening of foreign interest and travel that came as the century progressed. In the early 1820s the London Society for Promoting Christianity Amongst the Jews began to establish a foothold in Jerusalem, this early work leading to the installation of the first Anglican bishop in Jerusalem in 1842 and the dedication of Christ Church, the first Protestant church in Jerusalem, in 1849. The establishing of an Anglican bishopric in Jerusalem was an important element in the seventh Earl of Shaftesbury's lobbying for the large-scale return of the Jewish people to Palestine. He was related to Lord Palmerston, and played on the relationship in order to gain support for a cause in which Palmerston himself had little interest: 'he weeps not like his Master over Jerusalem, nor prays that now, at last, she may put on her beautiful garments'[8]. In 1839 the Church of Scotland had expressed its interest in the Jews of Palestine when Andrew Bonar, Robert Murray McCheyne and others set out on their 'Mission of Inquiry' to Palestine, in order to ascertain the conditions of Jews living there and the possibility of establishing a mission among them.[9] Interest in the history and archaeology of Palestine also embarked on its modern phase during this period with, most notably, the travels of the historical geographer Edward Robinson in and around the country, first in 1838 and again in 1853. Though a different kind of interest is represented by the travels of the artist David Roberts, his numerous sketches made during his visit to Egypt, Palestine and Syria in 1838–39 catered for a clientèle interested in the history of the area, and not least of the holy places of Palestine.[10] One might sum up the rest of the nineteenth century, on the Christian side, as a period of sustained pressure by some Christians to bring about the possibility of a Jewish state in Palestine. A significant part of the

---

[7] Cf. M. Vreté, 'The Restoration of the Jews in English Protestant Thought 1790–1840', *Middle Eastern Studies* 8 (1972), 3–50(5–6).

[8] Hodder, *The Life and Work*, 167 (diary entry for 1 August, 1840).

[9] See S.C. Reif, 'A Mission to the Holy Land – 1839', *Transactions of the Glasgow University Oriental Society* 24 (1971–2[1974]), 1–13.

[10] See *Yesterday and Today: The Holy Land. Lithographs and Diaries by David Roberts, R.A.* Text by Fabio Bourbon, Photographs by Antonio Attini (Shrewsbury: Swan Hill Press, 1997).

effort involved the encouragement of Theodor Herzl and others to believe that the restoration of Zion was indeed desirable and achievable.

The Biblical Promises

Now Israel-in-the-land is fact, and such are the implications and ramifications of this 'land question' that small-scale disturbances in Israel or West Bank, serious and even tragic though these are for those involved, can at any moment take media precedence over the deaths through war, famine or disease of hundreds of thousands in Africa. In addition to the intransigence that afflicts most disputes about territory, there is the further complication that the Israeli cause has advocates both Jewish and Christian who argue that the Genesis promises to the patriarchs in relation to the land are 'eternal' and irrevocable (cf. Gen. 13:14–17[15]; 17:4–8[8]; 48:4). In the relevant texts God appears to guarantee the fulfilment of his promises willy-nilly, with the perpetuation of the blessing conditional upon his own character rather than upon human compliance with any requirements specially attaching to the promises.[11]

There is no question that throughout the Old Testament the destiny of the people of Israel is closely bound to the physical land of Israel. Even when prophets and psalmists look to the more distant future of their people it is conceived in terms of their residing in the land. The New Testament, by contrast and for obvious reason, has no land dimension to its doctrine of the church, while in its conception of the church as ultimately a 'heavenly' reality it opens still wider the gap between the thought-world of the one Testament and the other.

There is the additional consideration that the Old Testament is concerned not only with land, but also with territorial expansion: basic to the whole concept of 'the land' is the idea of conquest and legitimized occupation of what originally belonged to others. Whatever the historical realities in any given period, Psalm 72:8, referring to the Davidic king, sums up a lot of hopes that find expression in the Old Testament: 'May he rule from sea to sea and from the River to the ends of the earth.' Read from the perspective of a benign messianic rule over the nations, the text has a certain

---

[11] P.R. Williamson, 'Promise and Fulfilment: The Territorial Inheritance', in P.S. Johnston and P.W.L. Walker (eds.), *The Land of Promise: Biblical, Theological and Contemporary Perspectives* (Leicester: Apollos, 2000), 15–34(23–24), suggests that, while the promise is unconditional, the conditionality attaches to the identity of those who actually hold the land.

glow about it. Still, nationalistic territorialism is a troublesome concept, and it is easy to portray ancient Israel to its disadvantage under this heading. This is not to suggest that Israel was in any way different from its neighbours in this respect. It is just that the similarity is the more surprising given the developed sense of morality and human dignity that we also find in the Old Testament, and that sets its texts apart from anything that other near eastern nations and cultures have bequeathed to us.

The Pentateuchal land promises may appear to be straightforward, but we must do them the favour of considering them against a broader biblical background than their immediate settings. We should note, in the first place, that expressions such as 'forever' and 'in perpetuity' are commonplace in ancient near eastern grants of land and of rights of succession, together with statements about inalienability of property or rights from individuals or their descendants.[12] The interpretative implications of this for Old Testament theology probably have still to be worked out; there are Old Testament texts for which the observation is doubtless important. The Rechabite episode in Jeremiah 35 is one such. It is relatively uncontroversial in theological terms. It ends with the divine promise that 'Jonadab son of Rechab shall never fail to have a man standing before me' (v. 19),[13] and it invites a question about the nature of its fulfilment.[14]

Perhaps most significantly, the Aaronide priesthood is said in the Old Testament to have been established on the basis of an eternal covenant. The underlying conception is expressed in Exodus 29:9, 'the priesthood is theirs by a perpetual ordinance', where *NIV* has 'by a lasting ordinance' for *l^{e}huqqat ^{c}ôlām*. This bestowal of perpetual priesthood is reaffirmed to Phinehas, of the Aaronide connection, in Numbers 25:10–13, following on Phinehas' intervention at Shittim: 'He and his descendants after him will have a covenant of priesthood for all time, because he was zealous for his

---

[12] Cf. Weinfeld, *The Promise of the Land*, 236–64.

[13] This promise is not linked to the continuation of the Jerusalem temple (*pace* Williamson, 'Promise and Fulfilment', in Johnston and Walker [eds.], *The Land of Promise*, 26n. 27).

[14] The importance of establishing the proper significance of biblical expressions denoting 'eternality' becomes very evident when we consider the fact that the Jewish people *qua* nation have spent much more time outside the land of Israel than in it. The addition of a thousand-year residence during 'the Millennium' would, on the usual sorts of calculation, tip the balance the other way, but would not eliminate the basic paradox. (Essentially the first of these two points is also made by Burge, *Whose Land?*, 118–19, with specific reference to Israelite-Jewish occupancy of Jerusalem.)

God and made atonement for the Israelites' (v. 13). In neither text is there any hint of conditionality, and in the second case the 'covenant' is given after blatant national apostasy at Shittim (Num. 25:1–3), which suggests that 'conditionality' has actually been outfaced in the Numbers exposition of this priestly covenant. That is why the Chronicler, probably writing in the fourth century, is even then reiterating the terms of the original 'Aaronic covenant': 'Aaron was set apart, he and his sons forever, to consecrate the most holy things, to make offerings before the Lord, to minister to him and to pronounce blessings in his name forever' (1 Chr. 23:13). This commitment to the Aaronide priesthood is given even more striking expression in Jeremiah 33:18: 'the Levitical priests will never lack[15] a man before me to offer up burnt offerings, to present cereal offerings, and to make sacrifices forever (*kl-hymym*)'. The terms of another verse in the same chapter, and their implications, certainly offer a challenge to literal fulfilment:

> Just as the host of heaven cannot be numbered and the sand of the sea cannot be measured, so I will multiply the descendants of David my servant and the Levites who minister to me. (v. 22)

On the other hand, 1 Samuel 2:30 pays its respects to the concept of an 'eternal' covenant with the priesthood and then appears to revoke this 'eternal' promise.

> Therefore the Lord the God of Israel declares, 'I promised that your house and your father's house would serve before me forever.' But now the Lord says, 'Far be it from me!'

In the light of our other texts it is no answer to say that Eli 'was living under the Mosaic economy, which was conditional in character'.[16] What appears to be happening in 1 Samuel 2:30–36 is that the promise is redirected, so that there is not, strictly speaking, a cancellation of the original terms. At the same time, the language is plainly that of revocation. The next paragraph may offer a clue as to how this tension has come about.

Nothing much is to be gained by questioning the expressions used in these various texts about 'eternal' or 'perpetual'

---

[15] Lit. 'there will not be cut off to the Levitical priests'; cf. the similar construction in Jeremiah 35:19, in relation to the Rechabites.

[16] So J.D. Pentecost, *Things to Come: A Study in Biblical Eschatology* (Grand Rapids: Zondervan, 1964), 78. It is a major defect in Pentecost's consideration of biblical covenant in relation to 'prophecy' that he has scarcely any discussion of the Mosaic covenant or of what may or may not be implied by 'conditionality'.

undertakings. If it is argued that 'perpetual' is too strong for the underlying Hebrew term *côlām* in Exodus 29:9, the same would have to apply to the Genesis land promises (cf. Gen. 13:15; 17:8), and their status as promises of perpetual land tenure would have to be scaled down accordingly. It is noteworthy, too, in this connection that the 'unconditional' covenant of Davidic kingship, set out in 2 Samuel 7, is qualified in yet other texts. The conditionality expressed in 1 Kings 2:3–4 (cf. Ps. 132:11–12) is, in effect, a restraining codicil to the main text in 2 Samuel 7. A similar qualification is introduced in the oracle in 1 Kings 9:3–9: the judgment of exile and destruction of verses 7–9 is contrasted with the possibility of Davidic rule over Israel 'forever' (v. 5). Bruce Waltke, among others, argues that even the 'unconditional' Abrahamic promise has been subjected to qualification in such a text as Genesis 18:19: 'For I have chosen him (sc. Abraham), so that he may direct his children and his house after him to keep the way of the Lord by doing what is right and just, so that the Lord may bring about for Abraham what he has promised concerning him.'[17] Indeed, the common distinction made between 'conditional' and 'unconditional' biblical covenants is possibly an oversimplification. Waltke's essay on conditional elements in unconditional covenants is followed in the same volume by another, by W.J. Dumbrell, that seeks to show that even the Sinai covenant has its *un*conditional dimension.[18] Dumbrell fairly notes that paradox abounds in the 'domain of biblical studies'.[19]

The second main point to be made is that there is clear indication in at least a couple of Old Testament passages that the Abrahamic land promise was regarded as having met its fulfilment in the historical period. 1 Kings 4–5 shows that, for one biblical writer, the reign of Solomon represented the fulfilment of territorial and other aspirations such as are found in the patriarchal promises in Genesis.

---

[17] See B. Waltke, 'The Phenomenon of Conditionality within Unconditional Covenants', in A. Gileadi (ed.), *Israel's Apostasy and Restoration: Essays in Honor of Roland K. Harrison* (Grand Rapids: Baker Book House, 1988), 123–39: 'YHWH explains that his grant extends only to those within Abraham's household who behave ethically' (129). Although Genesis 18:19 does not, of course, single out the promise of land as specially contingent on the behaviour of Abraham's descendants, the reference to them tends to push to the fore the question of their continued existence and possession of the land.

[18] W.J. Dumbrell, 'The Prospect of Unconditionality in the Sinaitic Covenant', in Gileadi (ed.), *Israel's Apostasy*, 141–55.

[19] Dumbrell, 'The Prospect', 142.

Judah and Israel were as numerous as the sand by the sea. They ate and drank and rejoiced. Solomon ruled over all the kingdoms from the River to the land of the Philistines, as far as the border of Egypt. They brought tribute and were servants of Solomon all the days of his life.

(1 Kgs. 4:20–5:1[4:20–21])

All the days of Solomon, Judah and Israel from Dan to Beersheba lived securely, everyone under their own vine and fig-tree.

(1 Kgs. 5:5[4:25])

Here, if correspondence of terms is anything to go by, there is at the very least *a* fulfilment of the promises to the patriarchs.[20] While the latter more often compare Abraham's progeny with the stars and the dust of the ground, sand features in Genesis 22:17 (cf. 32:12[13]). Moreover, Solomon's rule extends to the limits envisaged in the patriarchal promises.[21] Now, if this territory is given to Abraham and his descendants, according to Genesis 15:18–21, this is not to say that rule through client kings or the presence of subject peoples in their ancestral territory invalidates the cross-referring of 1 Kings 4–5 to Genesis 15. (Texts such as Gen. 22:17 which refer to the Israelites' possession of enemy cities may be said to have been 'fulfilled' in the Israelite occupation of Canaan.) And if latter-day advocates of an Old Testament-style land theology insist on a more comprehensive 'fulfilment' of Genesis 15:18–21, in which the descendants of Abraham occupy the whole region delimited in those verses, they will have to reckon with the displacement or elimination of the millions of non-Jews who inhabit the region, in an application, maybe, of the exterminatory 'ban' of the Old Testament that exceeds the bounds even of its biblical progenitor.[22] Even

---

[20] As Williamson notes, the Abrahamic promises are not fulfilled in the most comprehensive sense, in that the fulfilment under Solomon is short-lived ('Promise and Fulfilment', in Johnston and Walker [eds.], *The Land of Promise*, 31).

[21] Pentecost, *Things to Come*, 113–14, challenges this, quoting C.C. Ryrie.

[22] The prospect is faced head-on by J.N. Darby, the father of modern dispensationalism: 'The remnant of the Jews is delivered, and Antichrist destroyed; but the world, not yet acknowledging the rights of Christ, will desire to possess His heritage; and the Saviour must clear the land in order that its inhabitants may enjoy the blessings of His reign without interruption or hindrance, and that joy and glory may be established in this world, so long subjected to the enemy. The first thing, then, which the Lord will do will be to purify His land (the land which belongs to the Jews) of the Tyrians, the Philistines, the Sidonians; of Edom and Moab, and Ammon – of all the wicked, in short from the Nile to the Euphrates. It will be done by the power of Christ in favour of His people re-established by His goodness'

Deuteronomic law exercises a measure of discrimination in this regard, in distinguishing between near neighbours and those further afield (Deut. 20:16–18; cf. Josh. 9:3–27). A final point in relation to Solomon requires to be made. What we are considering is essentially a theological issue, and so questions as to whether or to what extent a Davidic-Solomonic kingdom in tenth-century Israel answered to the terms of 1 Kings 4–5, or whether the patriarchal promise tradition post-dates the time of David and Solomon, are relatively unimportant for our discussion.

Another text with strong fulfilment implications is Joshua 21:41–43(43–45). It lacks the specific detail of 1 Kings 4–5, and yet puts in a more comprehensive claim:

> The Lord gave to Israel all the land that he had sworn to give to their fathers, and they took possession of it and settled there.
>
> (Josh. 21:41[43])

> Not one of all the Lord's good promises that he made to the house of Israel failed; every one was fulfilled.
>
> (Josh. 21:43[45])

The same large claims are made in Joshua 23:14–16, which section also warns of the danger of ejection from the land in the event of apostasy:

> You know with all your heart and soul that not one thing has failed of all the good things that the Lord your God promised concerning you; all have come to pass for you, not one of them has failed. But just as every good promise that the Lord God has made to you has come true, so the Lord will bring on you all the evil, until he has destroyed you from this good land that the Lord your God has given you.
>
> (Josh. 23:14–15)

These statements are, of course, situated in a pre-monarchical context, following the settlement account of the book of Joshua. In the light of 23:14–16 it appears that the writer saw the fulfilment of the patriarchal promises as having taken place already in Joshua's lifetime. Moreover, since 'not one' of the good things that God promised had failed to materialize (21:43[45]), it would require

---

[22] (*continued*) (*The Collected Writings of John Nelson Darby*, II: Prophetic, I [ed. W. Kelly; London: G. Morrish, n.d.], 578 [The lecture, delivered in Geneva in 1840, is entitled, 'The Hopes of the Church of God in connection with the Destiny of the Jews and the Nations, as Revealed in Prophecy', 420–582]). Even the exclusivist Ezekiel knows more generous terms than these (47:22–23).

special pleading to limit 'the land' in 21:41(43) to something less than the land of the generous boundaries mentioned in the like of Genesis 15:18–21. In their own way, therefore, Joshua 21:41–43(43–45) and 23:14–16 are making at least as comprehensive a claim as 1 Kings 4–5, as far as the fulfilment of the patriarchal promises is concerned.[23]

New Testament Perspective

By contrast, there are parts of the New Testament that appear not to encourage the perpetuation of the people-land linkage that is commonplace within the Old Testament. When, for example, New Testament writers discuss Abraham, with whom the land promise begins, they move beyond this-worldly interpretations of the original promise. According to Romans 4:13, Abraham received a promise that he would 'inherit the world', which leaves the territorial limits of Genesis 15 and related texts looking somewhat jaded by comparison.[24] For the writer of Hebrews as well, the historical Abraham was rather more than a land-theologian: he looked for 'the city that has foundations, whose architect and builder is God' (Heb. 11:10). And we are told that Abraham and all those who, like him, were pilgrims and strangers on the earth were looking for a 'heavenly' country where God 'has prepared a city for them' (Heb. 11:16). The transposition of Old Testament expectation in a New Testament context can also be illustrated from the use made of Amos 9:11–12 in the account of the Jerusalem Council in Acts 15. The Amos text envisages the raising up of David's 'fallen tabernacle' – which language expresses the hope of the restoration of the kingdom of Israel and Judah, divided as it was after Solomon's

---

[23] These summary statements in Joshua 21 and 23 override such an interim report as Joshua 13:1–6, which mentions territory remaining outside Israelite control.

[24] Cf. T. Wright, 'Jerusalem in the New Testament', in P.W.L. Walker (ed.), *Jerusalem Past and Present in the Purposes of God* (2nd edn; Carlisle: Paternoster, 1994), 53–77(67). We might compare the way in which Josephus, interpreting the renewal of the Abrahamic promise to Jacob in Genesis 28:13–14 ('you will spread out to the west and to the east and to the north and to the south'), extends its range to embrace the whole earth: 'To them (sc. your descendants) I grant dominion over this land, and to their children who shall fill all that the sun beholds of land and sea' (*Ant.* 1:282; cf. 4:114–16). See Weinfeld, *The Promise of the Land*, 214–15. In talking of Sarah as a mother of nations, from whom kings would come, Genesis 17:16 seems to have implications for Old Testament territorial doctrine.

death – to its former greatness as in the days of David and Solomon. However, this land-locked prophecy is cited during the Council, by James the Jerusalemite church leader, as a prediction of that turning to God by Gentiles that had been taking place since Pentecost, and that had necessitated the convening of the Council (Acts 15:14–18). And if it is argued that this does not exhaust the content of the prophecy, the fact remains that there is no other citation of the Amos text in the New Testament.

The land dimension is also noticeably absent from New Testament passages, such as Romans 9–11 and Galatians 3,[25] in which the patriarchal promises are considered in the context of the Christian message. In Romans 9–11, which speaks of the ultimate blessing of Jewish people through the gospel, Paul seems to sideline the territorial question when discussing the problem of the promises in the light of majority Jewish rejection of Christ as Messiah. Nothing that he says about the future blossoming of Jewish faith in Christ implies a role for the land. We need to tread carefully here, to be sure, since there was still a land of Israel when Paul dictated these chapters, and, with his strong commitment to an imminent Parousia ('The night is far spent, the day is at hand', Rom. 13:12), he may have taken Jewish occupancy of the land for granted as he sought to reconcile Jewish rejection of Christ with the capacious promises to the patriarchs. His version of Isaiah 59:20, 'The deliverer will come *from* Zion' (quoted in Rom. 11:26), where the standard Hebrew text has '*to* Zion', could have implications for his understanding of the role, or non-role, of the land in relation to a future conversion of Jews, but it is difficult to tell.[26] W.D. Davies notes the further possibility that in Romans Paul may have avoided mention of the land out of political expediency, though he negates this point with his observation that no such explanation would account for the absence of the subject in Galatians.[27]

---

[25] Cf. Walker, 'The Land in the Apostles' Writings', in Johnston and Walker (eds.), *The Land of Promise*, 81–99(84). Walker also notes the spiritualizing implications of texts such as Romans 15:8(–9) and 2 Corinthians 1:20 in relation to the land (85). See further D. Mendels, *The Rise and Fall of Jewish Nationalism: Jewish and Christian Ethnicity in Ancient Palestine* (Anchor Bible Reference Library; New York: Doubleday, 1992), 243–75(258–62).

[26] For example, Paul could have thought of Zion in community terms.

[27] *The Gospel and the Land: Early Christianity and Jewish Territorial Doctrine* (Berkeley: University of California Press, 1974), 178–79. 'In writing to the Roman Church it might have been politically wise for the Apostle to avoid discussion of the question of the land. There is a probability that he was anxious not to cause any misunderstanding that might

Hermeneutical Issues

It might be concluded that some of the preceding discussion, for example of the texts in Joshua and 1 Kings, feeds the proposition that God owes nothing to the Jewish descendants of Abraham as far as land possession in the Middle East is concerned. Even if that were true, there remain, nonetheless, texts that on the face of it constitute major obstacles in the way of a thoroughgoing 'supersessionist' view on the land question. And it is here that we encounter a problem, in that a number of texts in the prophets (principally), that are understood 'futuristically' by many non-specialist readers of the Bible, tend to be explained by their specialist counterparts in relation to events and circumstances in the historical ('biblical') past. When, for example, prophets of the exilic age speak of a 'return' by the Judeans to their land, this may be read by the one side as a long-term prediction of developments in the last times, and by the other as expectation of the return of the Babylonian exiles, as happened in the late sixth century BC. Fundamental differences as regards principles of biblical interpretation are involved here, and they could not begin to be discussed adequately, much less conclusively, within the confines of this short study.

At the least, the conclusion seems unavoidable that the biblical writers wrote in accordance with the socio-political realities that they themselves experienced, and that they expressed their visions in terms and according to concepts already familiar to them and their contemporaries. Thus, even when they describe the 'ultimate future', their building blocks are the natural phenomena and the socio-political structures familiar from their own life experience. This can be illustrated from the future role predicted for the Assyrians in Isaiah 19, where they join with the Egyptians in the worship of the Lord, are to be a blessing on the earth together with Israel and Egypt, and are to be recognized by God as his 'handiwork' (Isa. 19:23–25). This never did happen, and there is a question as to how it could at any future date, since the Assyrians as such no longer exist. At the very least, some deft contemporizing of the text is required if fulfilment is to be achieved, and even then it would scarce qualify as 'literal fulfilment'. Of course, if we let go the literal categories that were necessary for the expression of the prophetic expectation in the first place, it is possible to hold on to the larger

---

[27] (*continued*) disturb Rome. Thus he used the phrase "The Kingdom of God" very sparingly for this reason. Political considerations did enter into Jewish-Christian relations in the first century. Paul counselled respect for the powers that be (Rom. 13: 1f.)' (178).

vision. No less than a James, as in Acts 15, might stand up and say that fulfilment came with the advent of the church and the conversion of the Gentiles! Other adaptations of the original 'vision' are, doubtless, also possible.

Literal fulfilment of biblical prophecy involves another kind of problem once we try to relate the biblical world to the much larger world that has to be considered at the beginning of the twenty-first century. For if we have problems with Assyrians, who are at least mentioned in the biblical text, what shall we say of such a major contemporary player as the United States of America, which has no part in the biblical tradition? The modern prophets, or modern interpreters of prophecy, have explained this absence in terms of the dissolution of the world's only remaining superpower because of moral corruption within or – an option currently not available – because of its submission to Communism. The latter explanation has, of course, played a diminishing role following the collapse of the Communist bloc in eastern Europe, and some quiet rearranging of the tea leaves has been going on, as Stephen Sizer has illustrated from two publications of Hal Lindsey, *The Late Great Planet Earth* (1970) and *Planet Earth 2000 A.D.: Will Man Survive?* (1994).[28] Yet, such is their love of country and flag that some North American commentators can occasionally be seen reclaiming a little for the beloved land: it will be bad in days to come, but not necessarily *really* bad.[29] However, the simple and obvious explanation of the biblical silence on North America is that the Old and New Testaments conceive their visions in terms of the world known to their writers; and some knew Assyria, and no one had heard of America, north or south.

The literalist approach has particular difficulty in handling certain future-oriented texts in Ezekiel 40–48 that deal with the reconstitution of the temple and its worship. Even some literalist-dispensationalist interpreters balk at the idea of a whole sacrificial system being restored – blood, gore, animal shrieks and all – in the expected Millennium. Not even when this regression into

---

[28] S.R. Sizer, 'Dispensational Approaches to the Land', in Johnston and Walker (eds.), *The Land of Promise*, 142–71(157–58).

[29] Cf. Lindsey himself in *The 1980's: Countdown to Armageddon* (Basingstoke: Lakeland/Marshall Morgan and Scott, 1983), 132: 'If some critical and difficult choices are made by the American people *right now*, it is possible to see the U.S. remain a world power. We could become an equal ally of the European confederation, with each dependent on the other. In that way, America would keep much of its sovereignty and freedom.' I do not have sufficient acquaintance with Lindsey's writings to know whether he thinks that the American people have complied.

superannuated ritual is explained as a looking back to the once-and-for-all offering of Christ does it appear convincing. The same interpreters would probably be the last to agree, but this revisiting of the doctrine of the atonement has more than a little in common with the traditional Roman Catholic teaching on the Mass, in which Christ continues to offer himself or to be offered, even while the attendant theology also subscribes, as it must, to the once-and-for-all character of his sacrifice at Calvary.

David Dolan, a popular writer on prophetic topics, more or less acknowledges the point of the preceding paragraphs in his book, *Israel in Crisis*:

> In terms familiar to him, Ezekiel seems to be outlining the main characteristics of the future kingdom of God, although a rebuilt temple is the focus of the prophecy. The book of Revelation later transforms these characteristics, including animal sacrifice, into more spiritual messages (21:10–22:5).[30]

Precisely. And unless we are happy to envisage the reinstitution of animal sacrifices, at God's behest, in a rebuilt temple in Jerusalem, we are bound to adopt a similar approach to the interpretation of certain Old Testament texts.

Whither Bound?

The foregoing discussion relates to the interpretation of biblical texts, not to the right of the state of Israel to exist. The latter point was settled by a vote of the United Nations on 29 November 1947, and the state was proclaimed on 14 May 1948. Now, while the New Testament, as we have seen, has little to say on the subject of 'land theology', its foremost theologian maintains that the Jewish people are the special object of God's mercy.[31] Paul's treatise on the subject in Romans 9–11 is clear in its assertion that 'all Israel will be saved' (11:26), and, in whatever sense this is intended, it is not fulfilled in the conversion of the Gentiles and the existence of the Christian church as at present.

---

[30] *Israel in Crisis: What Lies Ahead?* (Colorado Springs: House of David Publishers, 2001), 118.

[31] C.E. Armerding, 'Stewardship of the Land: A Christian Mandate', in Johnston and Walker (eds.), *The Land of Promise*, 215–31(229) suggests that, since for Paul the Jewish people are 'beloved' for the sake of their ancestors, so also the land in which God's saving events were acted out is deserving of honour, and this without respect to prophetic systems of interpretation.

a hardening has come upon part of Israel until the full number of the Gentiles comes in;

the gifts and calling of God are irrevocable.

(Rom. 11:25, 29)

Paul makes no mention of land, and the silence is probably signifi-cant.[32] Nevertheless, there are references in the New Testament that assume the land of Israel as the theatre of operation in that future with which prophecy is concerned. One of the most quoted is Luke 21:24 ('and Jerusalem will be trodden down by the Gentiles until the times of the Gentiles are fulfilled'), which appears to imply a res-toration of Jerusalem to Jewish sovereignty after a period of Gentile domination. At the same time, it is important to appreciate what the verse does not say – unless, that is, it is read against a background of interpretation that invests it with implications that exceed its imme-diate terms. Moreover, as with other features of the Lucan passage, it has to be read in the light of verse 32 and the statement that 'this generation will not pass away until everything has taken place'.[33]

In conclusion, it appears that New Testament writers addressing the question of Israel have their sights set on something more than the occupation of territory, for when biblical prophecies or prom-ises find answers that override and overtop the original terms of the prophecy or promise – heaven for a piece of earthly real estate, a divine messiah for a mortal Davidide – talk of failure of fulfilment is surely beside the point.

Apocalyptic Determinism

If the issue of literal vs symbolic is much rehearsed in discussions of biblical prophecy, the problem of determinism is less recognized but probably has greater practical consequences. There is the consider-able danger that the reader of the biblical text may come away with the idea that the future is all predetermined, the die is cast, and nothing that he or she can do will affect matters. This is essentially

---

[32] When, therefore, Paul is paraphrased as saying that 'the Lord will one day restore Israel to its place of favor and will fulfill the Old Testament promises to Abraham' (S. Ellisen, *Who Owns the Land?* [2nd edn; ed. C.H. Dyer; Wheaton: Tyndale House Publishers, 2003], 125), it is impor-tant not to read more than was intended into Paul's various references to Israel in Romans 9–11.

[33] There is, of course, the further consideration that, since Jerusalem 'undi-vided' has been in Israeli hands since 1967, the 'times of the Gentiles' must have come to an end a generation ago.

the problem of apocalyptic determinism, the effect of which is to discourage human initiative in favour of a fatalistic, quietistic attitude to one's own existence and to the world around. I want to illustrate the negative effects of apocalyptic determinism from a New Testament passage in which issues of geographical identity are involved.

In Revelation 17 the seer describes a woman seated on a scarlet beast that has seven heads, and on her forehead the legend, 'Babylon the great, mother of harlots and of earth's abominations' (v. 5). The woman, says the seer, is 'drunk with the blood of the saints and the blood of the witnesses to Jesus' (v. 6). The seven heads are explained as seven mountains, and also as seven kings (vv. 9–10), and most biblical commentators follow the 'preterist' view that identifies the woman with the Roman Empire under which the apocalyptist and his friends were already suffering because of their Christian faith.[34] Not so, however, a tradition of Protestant interpretation that sees here a foretelling of the rise of Roman Catholicism as heir to the traditions and the dominance of the Roman Empire. Revelation 17 thus becomes a prediction of the downfall of the Roman church.

As I have noted elsewhere,[35] this interpretation has itself in the modern period ridden on the back of a highly imaginative retelling of ancient history from Nimrod to Constantine that makes Roman Catholicism the complaisant heir of Babylonian religion and the Roman imperial cult. Alexander Hislop's *The Two Babylons*, first published in 1853[36] and the purveyor of this misinformation, combines fact and fiction in a way that has secured deuterocanonical status for it in some circles. Hislop took the equation of the woman and Roman Catholicism more or less for granted, but when we look for evidence that the woman of Revelation 17 has a specifically religious significance we look in vain. If the Roman Catholic church

---

[34] For the view that the woman of Revelation 17 was originally Jerusalem – a city *attacked by* Rome – see M. Barker, *The Gate of Heaven: The History and Symbolism of the Temple in Jerusalem* (London: SPCK, 1991), 49; cf. T. Wright, 'Jerusalem in the New Testament', in Walker (ed.), *Jerusalem Past and Present*, 71.

[35] 'The Two Minorities', *Priests and People* 7/1 (January 1993), 10–13(12).

[36] *The Two Babylons: Their Identity, and the Present Antichrist also the Last* (Edinburgh: William Whyte, 1853). The subtitle 'The Papal Worship proved to be the Worship of Nimrod and his Wife' appears in the second and subsequent editions (1858, 1862, 1871). The later editions represent a significant expansion of the original volume. Hislop mentions 'a very large accumulation of new evidence' (2nd edn, ix).

has spilled the blood of saints and witnesses to Jesus, and so fulfilled the terms of verse 6, so also have non-Catholics, and – more to the point – so did the Roman Empire. Much, therefore, has to be made of the language of harlotry in the chapter in order to sustain the religious interpretation. In the Old Testament, harlotry is used as a figure for spiritual defection from the God of Israel who had committed Israel to himself in a kind of marriage covenant (cf. Exod. 34:15; Deut. 31:16). Accordingly, it is assumed that the apocalyptic harlot, as the counterpart to the bride of Christ introduced in Revelation 19, must represent a debased form of Christianity that is in contrast with Christ's true church. But again our Hebrew Bible is a better guide, for there it is a relative commonplace to portray the cities of the east as harlot enterprises thriving on injustice and oppression. Tyre (Isa. 23:15–18), Samaria (Ezek. 23:5–8), Nineveh (Nah. 3:4), and even Jerusalem (Isa. 1:21) are all given the harlot treatment. There is no indication of anything different for the 'Babylon' of Revelation 17.

Bad Exegesis Costs Lives

It is the effect of the 'Two Babylons' interpretation on its sponsors that is specially important, for once one has made the equation between the apocalyptic Babylon and Roman Catholicism one is into the area of apocalyptic determinism. If Scripture portrays the judgment of this 'ecclesiastical Babylon' as already entered in the divine calendar, then one should not attempt to defend what God wills to destroy. Dialogue is thus ruled out, and those who are committed to this line of interpretation deny themselves the possibility of healthful influencing of those whom they regard as in error. Moreover, misinterpretation of biblical texts on this scale has, over the centuries, fed community tension and contributed to tragic waste of life. Both parties in the long history of relations between Protestants and Roman Catholics have been guilty of 'Bible abuse' of one sort or another, with appalling consequences. That a particular branch of Christendom has luminous sins to its account is, however, not to say that it stands under apocalyptic judgment, long since decreed and written down, and unavoidable.

Apocalyptic determinism is no less a factor to be reckoned with where the subject is Israel, its land and its future. In the face of prophetic 'inevitabilities' it becomes possible to interpret every development in the region as divinely foreordained, and such is the variety and the complexity of material in the biblical prophetic-apocalyptic canon that supporting texts can always be found, whatever the theory. That is one reason why the need is not for more books seizing on Bible passages with possible links to current volatilities in the Middle East, but for study of the appropriate methods by which prophetic and apocalyptic texts are to be read and interpreted. As time goes by and the predictions of the interpreters of prophecy do not necessarily come to pass, the desirability of this switch in emphasis will become more apparent, but that is no guarantee that the seriousness of the issues and the dignity of Scripture will meet with their deserved response.

Chapter Nine

'Neither on this mountain, nor in Jerusalem'

The transcending of geographical boundaries and of the very 'holy land' concept itself is a, perhaps surprising, feature of the story of Christ's encounter with the Samaritan woman at the well of Sychar, as recounted in John 4. The story is securely anchored in geographical detail that encourages thoughts of historical reminiscence. Christ is on the way north from Judea to Galilee and 'must needs go through Samaria' (v. 4, *AV*). If some purists regarded Samaria as profane territory to be avoided even at the cost of extra toil and travel, he is not so minded. Not many years later serious trouble resulting in Galilean fatalities erupted at the northern end of the route normally taken by Galileans on their travels between Galilee and Judea.[1] Nor does the Gospel writer himself stint on detailing the venerable associations of the place where Christ met the Samaritan woman. Sychar was 'near the piece of ground that Jacob gave his son Joseph' (v. 5; cf. Gen. 48:22; Josh. 24:32), 'Jacob's well was there' (v. 6; cf. v. 12), and 'our fathers worshipped on this mountain' (v. 20; cf. Josh. 8:33)[2] – the very Mount Gerizim which formed part of the scenic backcloth for the interview between Christ and the woman. Indeed, the wealth of patriarchal association in the early verses of the chapter encouraged W.D. Davies to talk of *two*

---

[1] Josephus, *Ant.* 20:118. Cf. Seán Freyne, *Galilee from Alexander the Great to Hadrian 323 B.C.E. to 135 C.E.: A Study of Second Temple Judaism* (Wilmington: Michael Glazier/Notre Dame: University of Notre Dame Press, 1980), 74, 219–20. We might also compare the poor reception of Christ in a Samaritan village 'because he was heading for Jerusalem' (Lk. 9:51–56). Josephus also comments (*Vita* 269) that the route through Samaria was essential for anyone wishing to make quick progress between Galilee and Judea.

[2] As is well known, the Samaritan Pentateuch words several Pentateuchal texts so that they support the Samaritan claim that Gerizim rather than Jerusalem was the place that God had appointed for the national shrine.

Samaritan holy places in the chapter, viz. Jacob's well and Gerizim.[3]

Good Samaritans

Christ's attitude to Samaritans is consistently represented in the Gospels as positive and welcoming. This is especially true of Luke's Gospel, and is illustrated at three different points. It is so in chapter 9 where Luke draws a parallel between Christ and Elijah, following on from the account of the Transfiguration.[4] When he prefaces the so-called 'Travel Narrative' section of his Gospel with a reference to the time when Christ would be 'taken up' (9:51), we are reminded of the introduction to Elijah's last journey in 2 Kings 2:1 ('When the Lord took Elijah up to heaven in a whirlwind'). The 'taking up' that Luke has in mind is doubtless the Ascension, which provides the final scene in his Gospel account (Lk. 24:50–53) and the first in his companion account of the early church (Acts 1:1–11). A possibly clearer allusion to Elijah at the time of his 'ascension' comes in verse 54. But this 'ascension' parallel sets up an ultimately more significant *contrast* between Elijah and Christ, for, whereas prior to his 'ascension' Elijah had been involved in calling down a judgment of fire on those sent to arrest him (2 Kgs. 1:10–12), Christ rebuked his disciples for proposing a similar fate for a Samaritan village that did not show him hospitality (Lk. 9:54–56).[5] In the next chapter, as if to reinforce the point, Luke has Christ tell the parable of the 'Good Samaritan' whose compassion for a victim of a bandit attack put a Jewish priest and Levite in the shade (10:25–37). Again, when ten lepers living in the borderland between Samaria and Galilee successfully begged Christ to help them, it is noted that the only one of

---

[3] W.D. Davies, *The Gospel and the Land: Early Christianity and Jewish Territorial Doctrine* (Berkeley: University of California Press, 1974), 298–99.

[4] In his account of the conversation on the Mount of Transfiguration Luke has already drawn a parallel between the exodus in the time of *Moses* and the death of Christ (9:31).

[5] A number of Mss at Luke 9:54 have a specific reference to Elijah: 'Lord, do you want us to command fire to come down from heaven and consume them, *just as Elijah did?*' (cf. *AV*). The last clause is generally regarded as secondary. However, the gloss, if such it is, only makes explicit the implied cross-reference to 2 Kings 1 that most readers would in any case recognize. Later, Luke himself is able to recount a more appropriate 'praying down' – of the Holy Spirit – upon a whole community of Samaritans who had responded to the Gospel (Acts 8:5–17[14–17]).

them who returned to express his gratitude was a Samaritan (17:11–19[16]).

Places of Worship

So in John 4 Christ comes to a Samaritan town called Sychar, near which is a well that tradition associates with the patriarchs Jacob and Joseph. At first the conversation with the Samaritan woman is about water and thirst, and then about the satisfaction of deeper-felt spiritual needs ('a spring of water welling up to eternal life', v. 14); but when the spotlight is shone on the woman's personal life she introduces the subject of worship and the rival claims of Jerusalem and Gerizim to host the true worship of the God of Israel. To her surprise, no doubt, Christ responded by denying the absolute claim of either place to such recognition (v. 21).

His statement is all the more striking because he accepts the woman's identification of him as a Jew[6] and makes the uncompromising assertion that 'salvation is from the Jews' (v. 22). This is an important statement in more than one respect, for it indicates that the critique of Judaism in the Fourth Gospel (e.g. 8:42–47) has to be seen as in some degree 'in-house criticism', and no more, or no less, 'anti-Semitic' than the denunciations of Israel and Judah by their own sons the prophets in the Old Testament period.[7] What Christ does is to introduce to the woman a concept of worship that is valid and 'true' (vv. 23–24) without the need of legitimization from any particular holy spot or shrine. He most certainly does *not* intend what Procopius of Caesarea attributes to him:

> When she asked him about the mountain he replied that a time would come when the Samaritans would no longer worship on this mountain, but that true worshippers would worship there.[8]

This may reflect the establishment of Christian worship on Gerizim in the Byzantine period, but not even Procopius should have regarded such a development as the fulfilment of John 4:21.

Christ also talks of worshipping God as 'Father' (vv. 21, 23), bringing the concept to the fore in a way that, while characteristically Christian, is true neither for the Old Testament nor for the

---

[6] He does this even to the extent of including himself among Jewish worshippers of God ('we worship', v. 22).

[7] Cf. R.P. Gordon, *Hebrews* (Readings: A New Biblical Commentary; Sheffield: Sheffield Academic Press, 2000), 27–28.

[8] *Buildings* 5:7:3.

literature of Palestinian Judaism in the pre-Christian period.[9] Christ even reverses the normal language of worship when he talks of the Father 'seeking' worshippers: the Old Testament quite frequently speaks of humans seeking the Lord in worship or in supplication (e.g. Pss. 24:6; 27:8; 105:3). This seeking by the Father, as has been noted by Montefiore, represents only a part of a larger concept, developed in the New Testament, of God actively seeking out lost humanity with a view to their reconciliation to himself.[10] Christ's own journey via Sychar may be seen as an episode in this very search.

In John 4 Christ also informs the woman that what he has described is not just for a time as yet unrealized: 'the hour is coming and is now present' (v. 23). The Fourth Gospel has already intimated the superseding of the temple, and by implication the temple mountain, when it envisages Christ as the sanctuary-in-person, the divine Word that 'tabernacled' among humanity (1:14), and his body as the temple that would be raised again after three days (2:19–22). But how does this expression of 'realized (or 'inaugurated') eschatology' relate to the Old Testament depictions of end-time worship at the mountain of the Lord in Jerusalem? We might respond to the question along 'dispensationalist' lines, distinguishing between Christian worship in the 'church age' and the attendance of the nations in Jerusalem during a millennial reign of Christ over a restored Israel and a renovated earth.[11] Or, we might conclude that the Old Testament prophets were simply expressing their insights in accordance with the structures and in the terms that were familiar to them. This large issue has been touched upon in chapter 8.

Exemplars of Faith

If the confession of 'Doubting Thomas' in John 20:28 makes of him a key witness to faith in the risen Christ, we shall not be surprised to find that the same Gospel also makes the Samaritan woman and her companions into something of an exemplar of faith response to

---

[9] For an example see Ecclesiasticus 51:10.

[10] C.G. Montefiore, *The Synoptic Gospels*, II (London: Macmillan, 1909), 985: 'The virtues of repentance are gloriously praised in the Rabbinical literature, but this direct search for, and appeal to, the sinner, are new and moving notes of high import and significance.' Cf. L. Morris, *The Gospel According to John* (New London Commentaries; London: Marshall Morgan and Scott, 1972), 271n. 61.

[11] Cf., for example, Zechariah 14:4–21, which is often cited within this interpretative construct.

Christ. This becomes clearer when the next episode, the healing of the nobleman's son (vv. 46–54), and the bridging paragraph (vv. 43–45), are taken into account. There the importance of miracles for the attitude of 'the Galileans' toward Christ is noted: they had seen all that he had done in Jerusalem 'at the festival' (v. 45). When he comes to Cana, we are reminded that it was there that he changed the water into wine (v. 46), so the topic of miracle-working is being kept to the fore. We are at least partly prepared, therefore, for the response of Christ to the distress of the nobleman pleading for help for his son: 'Unless you (pl.) see signs and wonders you (pl.) will not believe' (v. 48). A more general state of mind, rather than just the man himself, is being exposed in these words. This preoccupation with miracles as a prerequisite to faith contrasts with the story of the Samaritan woman. The extraordinary insight of Christ into her circumstances is crucial for her developing recognition of the person talking with her, but that is the limit of the 'miraculous' that the narrative unfolds. When Christ arrives at Sychar he is tired after his journey (v. 6); no miraculous power conducts him on his way unhindered by physical limitation or the constraints of climate and terrain. The disciples have gone off to buy food (v. 8); there is no miraculous provision for them or their master. The others in the village who respond positively to Christ (v. 42) do so because they have heard him for themselves, and in that respect their experience corresponds to that of the far larger circle of hearers whom the Fourth Gospel also has in mind (see 20:29, 31). The Samaritans' crowning affirmation of Christ as 'the Saviour of the world' (v. 42) also makes them spokesmen and paradigmatic for the wider world of those responding to the Gospel wherever it would be announced.

There is Hope for a Worshipper

Such recognition of Christ, somewhere in rural Samaria, as 'Saviour of the world', speaks in its own way to the question of worship in relation to 'the holy place'. In the first instance, salvation derives the more clearly from relationship with the one worshipped rather than from association with a place. So much may be implied in John 1:51 where Christ tells Nathaniel that in the future he will 'see heaven opened and the angels of God ascending and descending upon the Son of Man'. In the Genesis original of this reference the angels are ascending and descending upon the *sullām* ('staircase'?) that links Bethel with heaven (Gen. 28:12); in John 'place' has given way to 'person'.[12] This word that is for 'now' (v. 23) transcends the limits

---

[12] Cf. Davies, *The Gospel and the Land*, 299.

and the symbolism of the worship at the sacred place as it has been observed hitherto. Moreover, the associating of the divine presence with a special locale had further implications of 'sacred space' attaching to it. Tabernacle and temple by their layout and systems of 'graded holiness' distinguished between high priest, ordinary priests and laity in a hierarchy of ritual holiness that the Gospel sets aside.[13] Moreover, the symbolism of the later temple added further distinctions in the temple courts, which, though not in any biblical blueprint, nevertheless, with their 'Court of the Gentiles', 'Court of the Women' and 'Court of Israel', reflected a disabling hierarchism as far as right of access to the temple-based worship of the God of Israel was concerned.

In the new economy of worship and service, as expounded by Christ, this unlikely woman – unlikely because she was a woman, and a Samaritan, and unlikely for the kind of woman that she had been – finds an enhanced place as a worshipper and servant of the living God. We are told that the disciples were surprised on their return from their food errand to find that Christ was talking with *a* woman (v. 27). If they had known that the topics of conversation included the nature of the true worship of God they might have been surprised even more. But, whatever *some* rabbis may have thought of the usefulness of educating women in theology,[14] the Gospel tradition, again under the name of Luke, has given us the cameo of the sisters of Bethany and, in particular, of Mary who, like any disciple sitting at his master rabbi's feet receiving instruction (cf. Acts 22:3), sits at Christ's feet as no less truly his disciple, choosing to receive what 'will not be taken away from her' (Lk. 10:38–42[42]). The noble lineage continues in the New Testament via Mary Magdalene the 'apostle to the apostles' (Jn 20:17–18), Tabitha-Dorcas the disciple (Acts 9:36)[15] and Phoebe the deacon, a 'supporter (or

---

[13] This is perhaps most clearly seen in the use of *hagioi* ('saints'/'holy ones') in the New Testament to describe the members of the church on earth. Far from implying isolation and hierarchy, the word always has a plural reference, even in the one text that uses the singular 'saint' (Phil. 4:21, 'Greet every saint'). Cf. also 1 Peter 2:5, 9.

[14] 'Whenever a man engages in much talk with women he brings evil on himself and neglects the study of Torah and at his last inherits Gehenna' (m. Aboth 1:5). Specifically on the teaching of Torah to women, R. Eliezer observed: 'If anyone instructs his daughter in Torah it is as though he teaches her lechery' (m. Sotah 3:4). Historically, attitudes to women and their capacity for Bible study and its dissemination have been little better among many Christians.

[15] This is the only occurrence of the feminine form of the noun 'disciple' in the New Testament.

'patron') of many' (Rom. 16:1–2; cf. 1 Tim. 3:11;[16] Phil. 1:1[?][17]).
The Samaritan woman's discussion with Christ by the well at
Sychar had implications for her and her sister women that she
cannot have imagined at the time.

---

[16] The view that 1 Timothy 3:11 is dealing with women deacons and not
the wives of deacons avoids the oddity that the section would be giving
instructions to the wives of deacons, but not to the wives of overseers (see
vv. 1–7). In the New Testament 'deacon' implies service – probably of a
practical nature – rendered to the Christian community.

[17] Since Romans 16:1 designates Phoebe as a deacon, and 1 Timothy 3:11
probably also refers to women deacons (see previous footnote), it is quite
possible that 'deacons' in Philippians 1:1 includes women like Euodia and
Syntyche who had served with Paul in his missionizing and who may be
presumed to have continued in some such capacity in Philippi (Phil. 4:2).

An editorial note in *PEFQS* 1885 informs readers that General Gordon had sent his communications on Eden and Golgotha in note form, intending to write them up at a later point. However, his death at Khartoum made this impossible. The note also observes that Gordon's communications show that his views were 'based on other than purely scientific grounds'. The text and accompanying drawings are reproduced here because of their importance in relation to the identifying of 'Gordon's Calvary' and 'The Garden Tomb'.

Appendix

Eden and Golgotha
by General Charles Gordon, R.E.

I.

Position of Eden

I have formed a theory with respect to the position of Eden. I believe the Greek of the text respecting the parting of the main river of Eden into four other rivers can be read that four rivers united to form one great river.

In Genesis we have one river Euphrates given us: on it was Babylon. We have the Hiddekel, on which was Nineveh (*vide* Daniel), and which is the Tigris; these two unite and come down the Persian Gulf. We need to identify the Pison and Gihon. The Pison is the Nile, its meaning is "overflowing" and it flowed into the Red Sea before the Flood; it is connected with Egypt, which, like Nineveh and Babylon, oppressed Israel. The Blue Nile encompasses Havilah, where there is gold. Havilah was a grandson of Shem, his brothers were Ophir and Sheba, also connected with gold, and with Abyssinia; they went forth by Mesha (? Mecca), they crossed the sea, for Solomon got his gold from Ophir by sea. Where is the Gihon? There is the Brook Gihon south of Jerusalem, the Valley of Hinnom, where idolatrous practices went on; it therefore is also a spot whence Israel was oppressed. On this brook is Jerusalem; its flow, when it has any, is to the Dead Sea, its ravine is very deep, and could have been the bed of a river before the Flood. There is the difficulty of finding a ravine from the Dead Sea descending to the Gulf of Akabah through Wâdy Arabah, the Valley of Salt. By report, the watershed or flow of the Valley of Salt is towards the Dead Sea, and not towards the Gulf of Akabah. Is there any other ravine from the Dead Sea to the Red Sea by which the Gihon could meet the Nile in that Red Sea?

Allowing for the moment that the Pison is the Nile, and Gihon is the Brook Gihon, that they flowed into the Red Sea, and through the Gate of the World, Bab el Mandeb, we find by taking off the soundings of the Indian Ocean, that there are two clefts of 1,000 fathoms deep, joining near Socotra, and then going south, gradually deepening till they reach 2,600 fathoms, some 100 or 200 miles west of Seychelles.

> Seychelles is granitic, all other isles are volcanic.
> Aden, query Eden.
> Mussulman tradition places Eden at Ceylon.

I do not go into the question whether or not the Tree of Knowledge is not the *Lodoicea seychellarium*, and the Tree of Life the *Artocarpus incisa*, though for myself I do not doubt it.

I was two years in the neighbourhood of the sources of the Euphrates, Arax, Phasis, &c.; no flood could connect these rivers;—floods do not alter the features of a country with respect to high ranges.

II

Golgotha

1.   I last wrote to you giving the four rivers of Eden, one of which was the Gihon on which Jerusalem was. I do not know if I then mentioned it was the Tyropœon Valley, which conclusion I came to ere I came to Palestine.

2.   *Golgotha.* The morning after my arrival at Jerusalem I went to the Skull Hill, and felt convinced that it must be north of the Altar. Leviticus i, 11, says that the victims are to be slain on the side of the Altar northwards (literally to be slain slantwise or askew on the north of the Altar); if a particular direction was given by God about where the types were to be slain, it is a sure deduction that the prototype would be slain in some position as to the Altar: this the Skull Hill fulfils. With reference to the word "askew" or "aslant," we

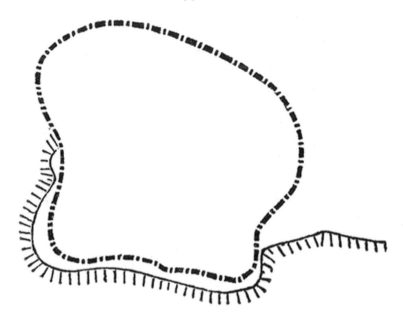

have the verse "all the day long have I stretched out my arms to a rebellious people" (Isa. lxv, 2). Draw a line from the centre of the Sakhra to the centre of the Skull; draw a perpendicular to this line, at centre of skull; a cross on that line will embrace all the city and Mount of Olives, and be askew to the Altar.

The Latin Holy Sepulchre is west of the Altar, and therefore, unless the types are wrong, it should never have been taken as the site.

I pass by the fact of the tradition of Beth hat Selzileh, of the precipice, of the tradition of its being the place Jeremiah wrote the Lamentations (which describes the scenes enacted there nearly 600 years afterwards, "Is it nothing to thee, all ye that pass by" (Lam. i, 12), &c., or the particularly suitable entourage of the place, for these things may be fanciful. I also will not hold to the fact that in the twelfth century St. Stephen's Church was at the Damascus Gate, outside, and St. Stephen was stoned nine months after our Lord's Crucifixion, and that it is unlikely that the Jews would have had two places of execution in nine months.

2.   And I will come to the more fanciful view, that the mention of the place of Skull in each four gospels is a call to attention. Wherever a mention of any particular is made frequently, we may rely there is something in it; if the skull is mentioned four times, one naturally looks for the body, and if you take Warren's or others' contours with the earth or rubbish removed showing the natural state of the land, you cannot help seeing that there is a body, that Schick's conduit is the

oesophagus, that the quarries are the chest, and if you are venturesome you will carry out the analogy further. You find also the verse (Ps. xlviii), "Zion, on the sides of the north;" the word "pleura," same as they pierced His *pleura*, and there came blood and water, God took a *pleuron* from the side of Adam, and made woman. Now the Church of Christ is made up of, or came from, His *pleura*, the stones of the Temple came from the quarries, from chest of figure, and so on; so that fixed the figure of body to the skull.

3.   Then by Josephus's account, as I read it, the Tower Psephinus was on the rocky point opposite the skull. Titus had his headquarters at the slaughter-house, 2 furlongs from the wall, viz., 300 to 400 yards, near the *corner* (note that corner, for it is alluded to in the 400 cubits broken down by Jehoash, king of Israel), and my placing of the walls and reading of Josephus would make his point of attack just where Schick's conduit enters the city east of Damascus Gate, or at the cisterns to east, where I think Agrippa's wall began. Mystically, the Roman Eagle should have gone at the Lamb of Zion by the throat, viz., Schick's conduit. However, I will not continue this, for if you please you can get the papers and plans from my brother. I would do them for you if you wish; I did them for Chaplin long ago. The camp of the Assyrians is the place where Nebuchadnezzar camped a month *after the fall of the city*, when he came to *burn the Temple*; it is this day which the Jews keep as the fast, not the day of *taking the city*.

4.   Naturally, after discerning *the figure*, the question arose of Mount Zion, and of the boundaries; by studying the latter with the Septuagint there seemed no reason *by Scripture* to consider Ain Haud the *Enshemesh*. Septuagint has Beth Samos, and near Jebel el Tell is Kh. el Sama. Again, Gihon (being the Tyropœon) is to gush forth, and as the skull is the Altar, it is thence the two rivers, one to the Dead Sea, the other to the Mediterranean, are to come. At last Moses's blessing to Benjamin came in, "he shall rest between His arms," not his shoulders; so thus I brought the boundary up Gihon to Kh. el Sama.

4.   Other reasons came to back this view,—

> Nehemiah mentions town of Furnaces.
> He also mentions throne of *Governor*.
> Josephus mentions women's towers.

The word "furnace" is derived from *fornex*, thence the connection. The tent Cozbi and Zimri went into was a *furnace*. Josiah broke down the high places built by Manasseh near the Gate of *Governor*, which were, no doubt, these same *furnaces*. Herodias lived at Jaffa Gate, and even to this day there are *furnaces* there I should think, for the troops are there.

This led to looking up the history of the Levites, &c., in Judges, of Gibeon, of mouldy bread, Nob, Gibeah of Saul, &c., and the result is as I have just noted, according to my ideas; but it is a matter of perfect indifference to us all, for these sites are in each of us.

During these studies, the potters' field comes up, and also the pool where Abner and Joab met, the field of the treacherous ones, and my idea is that round about the Serpent's Pool is the Tophet, Aceldama, Potters' field; that down the Valley of Hinnom is the Perez of David.

I will not bore you much longer than to say that, by my ideas,

Kuryet el Eneb is
- Kirjath-jearim
- Ramathaim-Zophim
- Armathaim
- Ramah, one of them
- Place of Saul's anointing
- Arimathæa
- Emmaus

and that Samuel was sacrificing to the Ark when Saul came to him.

Schick has been writing on these subjects for years, and he plaintively says, "but how *am I* possibly to advance other views now?" In reality, in writing on these sites, no man ought to draw any cheques on his imagination; he ought to keep to the simple fact, and not prophesy or fill up gaps. If one wrote under cognomen *a*, and altered under cognomen *ß* it would be all right; as it is now, a man under his own name cannot go right about face all at once. The Ark was built at Abu Shusheh by Noah, and floated up to Baris; only in A.D. 776 was it placed on Ararat, which is "*holy land.*" God said, "Go to a mountain I will shew thee," a mountain already consecrated by the resting place of the Ark. Noah offered on the rock his sacrifice. Look at Genesis and you will see (Gen. xi, 1), after the Flood they journeyed *eastward* to Shinar; you might go eastward from either Ararat or El Judi near Jesereb ebn Omar for ever before you reached Shinar. I will not bore you any longer, except to say that I think there are not many places far apart of interest in the Scripture way, and that these few are –

1. Nazareth and region of Tiberias.
2. Plain of Esdraelon.
3. Shechem.
4. Bethel.
5. Jerusalem.
6. Bethlehem.
7. Hebron.
8. Kuryet el Eneb, Philistia.
9. Jericho, Gilgal, Ammon and Moab, Dead Sea, Valley of Arabah.

C.G.

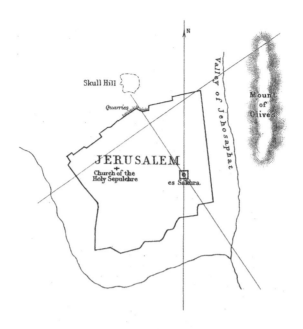

PLAN SHEWING POSITION OF THE TWO MOUNDS N. OF DAMASCUS GATE.

Bibliography

Abou-Assaf, A., Bordreuil, P., Millard, A.R., *La Statue de Tell Fekherye et son inscription bilingue assyro-araméenne* (Études Assyriologiques, 7; Paris: Éditions Recherche sur les Civilisations, 1982).

Ackroyd, P.R., *The Second Book of Samuel* (The Cambridge Bible Commentary; Cambridge: Cambridge University Press, 1977).

Alexander, P.S., 'Jerusalem as the *Omphalos* of the World: On the History of a Geographical Concept', in L.I. Levine (ed.), *Jerusalem: Its Sanctity and Centrality to Judaism, Christianity, and Islam* (New York: Continuum, 1999), 104-19.

Alexander, T.D., 'Beyond Borders: The Wider Dimensions of Land', in P.S. Johnston and P.W.L. Walker (eds.), *The Land of Promise: Biblical, Theological and Contemporary Perspectives* (Leicester: Apollos, 2000), 35-50.

Amichai, Yehuda, *Achshav Bara'ash: Shirim 1963-1968* (Tel-Aviv: Schocken, 1971).

Amit, Y., *Hidden Polemics in Biblical Narrative* (tr. J. Chipman; Biblical Interpretation Series, 25; Leiden: Brill, 2000).

_____, 'The Status of Jerusalem in the Pentateuchal Writings' (Heb.), in M. Garsiel, S. Vargon, A. Frisch, J. Kugel (eds.), *Studies in Bible and Exegesis*, 5 (Fs U. Simon; Ramat Gan: Bar Ilan University Press, 2000), 41-57.

Armerding, C.E., 'Stewardship of the Land: A Christian Mandate', in P.S. Johnston and P.W.L. Walker (eds.), *The Land of Promise: Biblical, Theological and Contemporary Perspectives* (Leicester: Apollos, 2000), 215-31.

Barker, M., *The Gate of Heaven: The History and Symbolism of the Temple in Jerusalem* (London: SPCK, 1991).

Barré, M.L., 'The Seven Epithets of Zion in Ps 48,2-3', *Biblica* 69 (1988), 557-63.

Beentjes, P., 'Jerusalem in the Book of Chronicles', in M. Poorthuis and Ch. Safrai (eds.), *The Centrality of Jerusalem: Historical Perspectives* (Kampen: Kok Pharos, 1996), 15-28.

Bennett, W.H., *Genesis* (Century Bible; London: Caxton, nd).

Bergler, S., 'Jesus, Bar Kochba und das messianische Laubhüttenfest', *JSJ* 29 (1998), 143-91.

Biddle, M., *The Tomb of Christ* (Stroud: Sutton Publishing, 1999).

Biran, A., 'To the God who is in Dan', in A. Biran (ed.), *Temples and High Places in Biblical Times* (Jerusalem: Hebrew Union College-Jewish Institute of Religion, 1981), 142-51.

Block, D.I., *The Book of Ezekiel: Chapters 25-48* (Grand Rapids/Cambridge: Eerdmans, 1998).

Bowman, G., '"Mapping History's Redemption": Eschatology and Topography in the *Itinerarium Burdigalense*', in L.I. Levine (ed.), *Jerusalem: Its Sanctity and Centrality to Judaism, Christianity, and Islam* (New York: Continuum, 1999), 163-87.

Bruce, F.F., 'Paul and Jerusalem', *Tyndale Bulletin* 19 (1968), 3-25.

Burge, G.M., *Whose Land? Whose Promise? What Christians Are Not Being Told about Israel and the Palestinians* (Carlisle: Paternoster Press, 2003).

Buss, M., 'The Psalms of Asaph and Korah', *JBL* 82 (1963), 382-92.

Cassuto U., *A Commentary on the Book of Genesis* [Heb.] (5th edn; Jerusalem: Magnes Press, 1969).

_____, 'Jerusalem in the Pentateuch', in *Biblical and Oriental Studies*, I: *Bible* (Jerusalem: Magnes Press, 1973), 71-78.

Childs, B.S., *Isaiah* (Old Testament Library; Louisville: Westminster John Knox, 2001).

Civil, M., 'The Sumerian Flood Story', in W.G. Lambert and A.R. Millard (eds.), *Atra-ḫasis: The Babylonian Story of the Flood* (Oxford: Clarendon Press, 1969), 138-45.

Clifford, R.J., *The Cosmic Mountain in Canaan and the Old Testament* (Harvard Semitic Monographs, 4; Cambridge, MA: Harvard University Press, 1972).

Clines, D.J.A., 'Sacred Space, Holy Places and Suchlike', in *On the Way to the Postmodern: Old Testament Essays, 1967-1998. Volume II* (SJSOT 293; Sheffield: Sheffield Academic Press, 1998), 542-54.

Cohn, R.L., 'The Mountains and Mount Zion', *Judaism* 26 (1977), 97-115.

_____, *The Shape of Sacred Space: Four Biblical Studies* (American Academy of Religion Studies in Religion, 23; Chico: Scholars Press, 1981).

Conder, C.R., *Tent Work in Palestine: A Record of Discovery and Adventure* (London: Richard Bentley, 1878).

Crombie, K., *For the Love of Zion: Christian Witness and the Restoration of Israel* (London: Hodder and Stoughton, 1991).

Dalman, G., *Sacred Sites and Ways: Studies in the Topography of the Gospels* (tr. P.P. Levertoff; London: SPCK, 1935).

Damrosch, D., *The Narrative Covenant: Transformations of Genre in the Growth of Biblical Literature* (San Francisco: Harper and Row, 1987).

Darby, J.N., *The Collected Writings of John Nelson Darby*, II: Prophetic, I (ed. W. Kelly; London: G. Morrish, n.d.).

Daube, D., 'Two Jewish Prayers', *Rechtshistorisches Journal* 6 (1987), 185-94.

Davies, W.D., *The Gospel and the Land: Early Christianity and Jewish Territorial Doctrine* (Berkeley: University of California Press, 1974).

———, *The Setting of the Sermon on the Mount* (Brown Judaic Studies, 186; Atlanta: Scholars Press, 1989).

Day, J., *God's Conflict with the Dragon and the Sea: Echoes of a Canaanite Myth in the Old Testament* (University of Cambridge Oriental Publications, 35; Cambridge: Cambridge University Press, 1982).

———, *Psalms* (Old Testament Guides; Sheffield: Sheffield Academic Press, 1990).

DeVries, S.J., *Yesterday, Today and Tomorrow: Time and History in the Old Testament* (Grand Rapids: Eerdmans, 1975).

Dolan, David, *Israel in Crisis: What Lies Ahead?* (Colorado Springs: House of David Publishers, 2001).

Donaldson, T.L., 'Proselytes or "Righteous Gentiles"? The Status of Gentiles in Eschatological Pilgrimage Patterns of Thought', *JSP* 7 (1990), 3-27.

Dumbrell, W.J., 'The Prospect of Unconditionality in the Sinaitic Covenant', in A. Gileadi (ed.), *Israel's Apostasy and Restoration: Essays in Honor of Roland K. Harrison* (Grand Rapids: Baker Book House, 1988), 141-55.

Ellisen, S., *Who Owns the Land?* (2nd edn; ed. C.H. Dyer; Wheaton: Tyndale House Publishers, 2003).

Elm, Susanna, 'Perceptions of Jerusalem Pilgrimage as Reflected in Two Early Sources on Female Pilgrimage (3rd and 4th Centuries A.D.)', *Studia Patristica* 20 (1989), 219-23.

Elnes, E.E., 'Creation and Tabernacle: The Priestly Writer's "Environmentalism"', *Horizons in Biblical Theology* 16 (1994), 144-55.

Elton, Lord, *General Gordon* (London: Collins, 1954).

Emerton, J.A., 'New Light on Israelite Religion: The Implications of the Inscriptions from Kuntillet 'Ajrud', *ZAW* 94 (1982), 2-20.

———, 'The Site of Salem, the City of Melchizedek (Genesis xiv 18)', *SVT* 41 (1990), 45-71.

Engemann, J., 'Das Jerusalem der Pilger, Kreuzauffindung und Wallfahrt', in *Akten des XII. Internationalen Kongresses für christliche Archäologie*, I (Jahrbuch für Antike und Christentum Ergänzungsband, 20, 1; Münster: Aschendorffsche Verlagsbuchhandlung, 1995), 24-35.

Farmer, W.R., 'The Geography of Ezekiel's River of Life', *BA* 19 (1956), 17-22.

Fishbane, M. *Text and Texture: Close Readings of Selected Biblical Texts* (New York: Schocken, 1979).

Frank, Georgia A., 'Pilgrim's Experience and Theological Challenge: Two Patristic Views', in *Akten des XII. Internationalen Kongresses für christliche Archäologie*, II (Jahrbuch für Antike und Christentum Ergänzungsband, 20, 2; Münster: Aschendorffsche Verlagsbuchhandlung, 1995), 787-91.

Frank, R.W., 'Pilgrimage and Sacral Power', in Barbara N. Sargent-Baur (ed.), *Journeys Toward God: Pilgrimage and Crusade* (Occasional Studies Series, 5; Kalamazoo, MI: SMC XXX Medieval Institute Publications, Western Michigan University, 1992), 31-43.

Frankfort, H., *Kingship and the Gods: A Study of Ancient Near Eastern Religion as the Integration of Society and Nature* (Chicago: University of Chicago Press, 1948).

French, Dorothea R., 'Journeys to the Center of the Earth: Medieval and Renaissance Pilgrimages to Mount Calvary', in Barbara N. Sargent-Baur (ed.), *Journeys Toward God: Pilgrimage and Crusade* (Occasional Studies Series, 5; Kalamazoo, MI: SMC XXX Medieval Institute Publications, Western Michigan University, 1992), 45-81.

_____, 'Mapping Sacred Centers: Pilgrimage and the Creation of Christian Topographies in Roman Palestine', *Akten des XII. Internationalen Kongresses für christliche Archäologie* (Jahrbuch für Antike und Christentum Ergänzungsband, 20, 2; Münster: Aschendorffsche Verlagsbuchhandlung, 1995), 792-97.

Freyne, Seán, *Galilee from Alexander the Great to Hadrian 323 B.C.E. to 135 C.E.: A Study of Second Temple Judaism* (Wilmington: Michael Glazier/Notre Dame: University of Notre Dame Press, 1980).

Friedman, M., 'Jewish Pilgrimage after the Destruction of the Second Temple', in N. Rosovsky (ed.), *City of the Great King: Jerusalem from David to the Present* (Cambridge, MA: Harvard University Press, 1996), 136-46.

Gerstenberger, E.S., *Psalms: Part 1, With an Introduction to Cultic Poetry* (The Formation of the Old Testament Literature, 14; Grand Rapids: Eerdmans, 1988).

Gobat, Samuel, *Samuel Gobat, Bishop of Jerusalem: His Life and Work. A Biographical Sketch, Drawn Chiefly from His Own Journals* (London: James Nisbet, 1884).

Goodman, M., 'The Pilgrimage Economy of Jerusalem in the Second Temple Period', in L.I. Levine (ed.), *Jerusalem: Its Sanctity and Centrality to Judaism, Christianity, and Islam* (New York: Continuum, 1999), 69-76.

Gordon, Charles, *Reflections in Palestine. 1883* (London: Macmillan, 1884).

_____, 'Eden and Golgotha', *PEFQS* 1885, 78-81.

_____, *Letters of General C.G. Gordon to his Sister M.A. Gordon* (London: Macmillan, 1888).

Gordon, R.P., 'The Targumists as Eschatologists', *SVT* 29 (1978), 113-30.

_____, 'Terra Sancta and the Territorial Doctrine of the Targum to the Prophets', in J.A. Emerton and S.C. Reif (eds.), *Interpreting the Hebrew Bible: Essays in honour of E.I.J. Rosenthal* (University of Cambridge Oriental Publications, 32; Cambridge: Cambridge University Press, 1982), 119-31.

_____, 'Inscribed Pots and Zechariah XIV 20-1', *VT* 42 (1992), 120-23.

_____, 'The Two Minorities', *Priests and People* 7/1 (January 1993), 10-13.

_____, 'The Ideological Foe: The Philistines in the Old Testament' (in forthcoming Festschrift in honour of Kevin J. Cathcart).

Goulder, M.D., *The Psalms of the Sons of Korah* (SJSOT 20: Sheffield: JSOT Press, 1982).

Grabbe, L.L., 'Sup-urbs or only Hyp-urbs? Prophets and Populations in Ancient Israel and Socio-historical Method', in L.L. Grabbe and R.D. Haak (eds.), *'Every City shall be Forsaken': Urbanism and Prophecy in Ancient Israel and the Near East* (SJSOT 330; Sheffield: Sheffield Academic Press, 2001), 95-123.

Greenfield, J.C., 'The Seven Pillars of Wisdom (Prov. 9:1) – A Mistranslation', *JQR* 76 (1985), 13-20.

Grotenhuis, Elizabeth ten, *Japanese Mandalas: Representations of Sacred Geography* (Honolulu: University of Hawaii, 1999).

Hadley, J.M., *The Cult of Asherah in Ancient Israel and Judah: Evidence for a Hebrew Goddess* (University of Cambridge Oriental Publications, 57; Cambridge: Cambridge University Press, 2000), 121-29.

Hall, S.G. (ed.), *Melito of Sardis: On Pascha and Fragments* (Oxford Early Christian Texts; Oxford: Clarendon, 1979).

Hallo, W.W., *Origins: The Ancient Near Eastern Background of Some Modern Western Institutions* (Studies in the History and Culture of the Ancient Near East, 6; Leiden: E.J. Brill, 1996).

Hanson, P.D., 'Zechariah 9 and the Recapitulation of an Ancient Ritual Pattern', *JBL* 92 (1973), 37-59.

_____, *The Dawn of Apocalyptic: The Historical and Sociological Roots of Jewish Apocalyptic Eschatology* (Philadelphia: Fortress Press, 1975).

Harvey, A.E., 'Melito and Jerusalem', *JTS* NS 17 (1966), 401-404.

Hislop, Alexander, *The Two Babylons: Their Identity, and the Present Antichrist also the Last* (Edinburgh: William Whyte, 1853).

Hodder, E., *The Life and Work of the Seventh Earl of Shaftesbury, K.G.* (Popular edn; London: Cassell, 1888).

Holden, J. Stuart, *The Master and His Men* ([repr.] Belfast: Ambassador Publications, 2002).

Holum, K.G., 'Hadrian and St. Helena: Imperial Travel and the Origins of Christian Holy Land Pilgrimage', in R. Ousterhout (ed.), *The Blessings of Pilgrimage* (Illinois Byzantine Studies, 1; Urbana and Chicago: University of Illinois Press, 1990), 66-81.

Horowitz, W., 'The Babylonian Map of the World', *Iraq* 50 (1988), 147-65.

_____, *Mesopotamian Cosmic Geography* (Mesopotamian Civilizations, 8; Winona Lake: Eisenbrauns, 1998).

Hunt, E.D., *Holy Land Pilgrimage in the Later Roman Empire AD 312-460* (Oxford: Clarendon, 1982).

Hurowitz, V., *I Have Built You an Exalted House: Temple Building in the Bible in Light of Mesopotamian and Northwest Semitic Writings* (SJSOT 115; JSOT/ASOR Monograph Series, 5; Sheffield: Sheffield Academic Press, 1992).

Hyamson, A.M. (ed.), *The British Consulate in Jerusalem in Relation to the Jews of Palestine 1838-1914*, I (Publications of the Jewish Historical Society of England; London: Edward Goldston, 1939).

Jacobsen, T., *The Sumerian King List* (Assyriological Studies, 11; Chicago: University of Chicago Press, 1939).

_____, *Kingship and the Gods: A Study of Ancient Near Eastern Religion as the Integration of Society and Nature* (Chicago: University of Chicago Press, 1948).

_____, 'The Eridu Genesis', *JBL* 100 (1981), 513-29.

Jellinek, A., *Bet-ha-Midrasch*, V (Vienna: Winter, 1873).

Jenson, P.P., *Graded Holiness: A Key to the Priestly Conception of the World* (SJSOT 106; Sheffield: JSOT Press, 1992).

Jeremias, Joachim, *Golgotha* (ΑΓΓΣΛΟΣ 1; Leipzig: Eduard Pfeiffer, 1926).

Johnson, A.R., *The Cultic Prophet in Ancient Israel* (2nd edn; Cardiff: University of Wales Press, 1962).

Joosten, J., *People and Land in the Holiness Code: An Exegetical Study of the Ideational Framework of the Law in Leviticus 17-26* (SVT 67; Leiden: E.J. Brill, 1996).

Keel, O., *The Symbolism of the Biblical World: Ancient Near Eastern Iconography and the Book of Psalms* (tr. T.J. Hallett; New York: Seabury Press, 1978).

Kessler, M., *Battle of the Gods: The God of Israel Versus Marduk of Babylon. A Literary/Theological Interpretation of Jeremiah 50-51* (Studia Semitica Neerlandica; Assen: Royal Van Gorcum, 2003).

Kissane, E.J., *The Book of Psalms Translated from a Critically Revised Hebrew Text*, I (Dublin: Browne and Nolan, 1953).

Klatzker, D., 'Sacred Journeys: Jerusalem in the Eyes of American Travelers before 1948', in Y. Ben-Arieh and M. Davis (eds.), *Jerusalem in the Mind of the Western World, 1800-1948* (With Eyes Toward Zion, 5; Westport: Praeger, 1997), 47-58.

Knox, Ronald, *The Holy Bible: A Translation from the Latin Vulgate in the Light of the Hebrew and Greek Originals* (London: Burns and Oates, 1949).

Korp, Maureen, *The Sacred Geography of the American Mound Builders* (Native American Studies, 2; Lewiston/Lampeter: Edwin Mellen Press, 1990).

Kraus, H.-J., *Psalmen*, I (BKAT 15/1; Neukirchen: Neukirchener Verlag, 1960).

Lang, B., *The Hebrew God: Portrait of an Ancient Deity* (New Haven and London: Yale University Press, 2002).

Laato, A., *'About Zion I will not be Silent': The Book of Isaiah as an Ideological Unity* (CBOTS 44; Stockholm: Almqvist and Wiksell, 1998).

Lane, Belden C., *Landscapes of the Sacred: Geography and Narrative in American Spirituality* (Isaac Hecker Studies in Religion and American Culture; New York: Paulist Press, 1988).

Lebon, J., 'Athanasiana Syriaca II: Une Lettre Attribuée à Saint Athanase d'Alexandrie', *Le Muséon* 41 (1928), 169-216.

Lemaire, A., 'Prières en temps de crise: les inscriptions de Khirbet Beit Lei', *RB* 83 (1976), 558-68.

Leupold, H.C., *Exposition of the Psalms* (London: Evangelical Press, 1972).

Levenson, J., *Sinai and Zion: An Entry into the Jewish Bible* (New Voices in Biblical Studies; Minneapolis: Winston Press, 1985).

Lichtenberger, H., '"Im Lande Israel zu wohnen wiegt alle Gebote der Tora auf": Die Heiligkeit des Landes und die Heiligung des Lebens', in R. Feldmeier and U. Heckel (eds.), *Die Heiden: Juden, Christen und das Problem des Fremden* (WUNT 70; Tübingen: J.C.B. Mohr (Paul Siebeck), 1994), 92-107.

Lightfoot, J.B., *The Apostolic Fathers* (2nd edn; II, 3 [London: Macmillan, 1889]).

Lindsey, H., *The 1980's: Countdown to Armageddon* (Basingstoke: Lakeland, 1983).

Lovell, E., *A Green Hill Far Away: The Life of Mrs C.F. Alexander* (Dublin: APCK/London: SPCK, 1970).

Lundbom, J.R., *Jeremiah 1-20: A New Translation with Introduction and Commentary* (AB 21A; New York: Doubleday, 1999).

Machinist, P., 'The Question of Distinctiveness in Ancient Israel: An Essay', in M. Cogan and I. Eph'al (eds.), *Ah, Assyria ... Studies in Assyrian History and Ancient Near Eastern Historiography Presented to Hayim Tadmor* (=*Scripta Hierosolymitana*, 33; Jerusalem: Magnes Press, 1991).

Margalioth, M., *Halakhoth on the Land of Israel from the Genizah* (Heb.) (Jerusalem: Mossad Harav Kook, 1973).

Mathews, K.A., *Genesis 1-11:26* (The New American Commentary, 1A; npl: Broadman and Holman, 1996).

McBride, S. Dean, 'Divine Protocol: Genesis 1:1-2:3 as Prologue to the Pentateuch', in W.P. Brown and S.D. McBride (eds.), *God Who Creates: Essays in Honor of W. Sibley Towner* (Grand Rapids: Eerdmans, 2000), 3-41.

McCauley, L.P., and Stephenson, A.A., (eds.), *The Works of Saint Cyril of Jerusalem*, 2 (Washington: Catholic University of America Press, 1970).

McKane, W., *Jeremiah*, II (ICC; Edinburgh: T & T Clark, 1996).

Mendels, D., 'Hecataeus of Abdera and a Jewish "patrios politeia" of the Persian Period (Diodorus Siculus XL,3)', *ZAW* 95 (1983), 96-10.

_____, *The Rise and Fall of Jewish Nationalism: Jewish and Christian Ethnicity in Ancient Palestine* (Anchor Bible Reference Library; New York: Doubleday, 1992), 243-75.

Menuhin, M., *The Decadence of Judaism in our Time* (Beirut: The Institute for Palestine Studies, 1965 [1969]).

Merrill, E.H., 'Pilgrimage and Procession: Motifs of Israel's Return', in A. Gileadi (ed.), *Israel's Apostasy and Restoration: Essays in Honor of Roland K. Harrison* (Grand Rapids: Baker, 1988), 261-72.

Meyers, C.L., and Meyers, E.M., *Zechariah 9-14: A New Translation with Introduction and Commentary* (AB 25C; New York: Doubleday, 1993).

Millard, A.R., and Bordreuil, P., 'A Statue from Syria with Assyrian and Aramaic Inscriptions', *BA* 45 (1982), 135-41.

Moberly, R.W.L., Review of R.S. Hendel, *The Text of Genesis 1-11: Textual Studies and Critical Edition* (1998), in *JTS* NS 51 (2001), 188-90.

Montefiore, C.G., *The Synoptic Gospels*, II (London: Macmillan, 1909).

Morgenstern, J., 'Psalm 48', *HUCA* 16 (1941), 1-95.

Murphy-O'Connor, J., 'Pre-Constantinian Christian Jerusalem', in A. O'Mahony (ed.), with G. Gunner and K. Hintlian, *The Christian Heritage in the Holy Land* (London: Scorpion Cavendish, 1995), 13-21.

Naveh, J., 'Old Hebrew Inscriptions in a Burial Cave', *IEJ* 13 (1963), 74-92.

Newton, Richard, *Rambles in Bible Lands* (London: Charles H. Kelly, 1891).

Nickle, K.F., *The Collection: A Study in Paul's Strategy* (Studies in Biblical Theology, 48; London: SCM Press, 1966).

Nissinen, M., 'City as Lofty as Heaven: Arbela and Other Cities in Neo-Assyrian Prophecy', in L.L. Grabbe and R.D. Haak (eds.), *'Every City shall be Forsaken': Urbanism and Prophecy in Ancient Israel and the Near East* (SJSOT 330; Sheffield: Sheffield Academic Press, 2001), 172-209.

Noth, M., 'Der Wallfahrtsweg zum Sinai (4. Mose 33)', *Palästinajahrbuch* 36 (1940), 5-28.

Oulton, J.E.L., 'Rufinus's Translation of the Church History of Eusebius', *JTS* 30 (1928-29), 150-74.

Pelletier A. (ed.), *Lettre d'Aristée à Philocrate* (Sources Chrétiennes, 89; Paris: Éditions du Cerf, 1962).

Pentecost, J.D., *Things to Come: A Study in Biblical Eschatology* (Grand Rapids: Zondervan, 1964).

Perowne, J.J.S., *The Book of Psalms* (6th edn; London: George Bell, 1888).

Peters, J.P., *The Psalms as Liturgies* (London: Hodder and Stoughton, 1922).

Polley, M.E., *Amos and the Davidic Empire: A Socio-Historical Approach* (New York/Oxford: Oxford University Press, 1989).

Pollock, J., *Gordon: The Man Behind the Legend* (London: Constable, 1993).

Pope, M.H., *El in the Ugaritic Texts* (SVT 2; Leiden: E.J. Brill, 1955).

Pulikottil, P., *Transmission of Biblical Texts in Qumran: The Case of the Large Isaiah Scroll 1QIsa^a* (Journal for the Study of the Pseudepigrapha Supplement Series, 34; Sheffield: Sheffield Academic Press, 2001).

Pullan, Wendy, 'Mapping Time and Salvation: Early Christian Pilgrimage to Jerusalem', in G.D. Flood (ed.), *Mapping Invisible Worlds* (Cosmos 9; Edinburgh: Edinburgh University Press, 1993), 23-40.

Qimron, E., and Strugnell, J. (eds.), *Qumran Cave 4: V, Miqsat Ma'ase Ha-Torah* (DJD 10; Oxford: Clarendon, 1994).

Rad, G. von, *Genesis: A Commentary* (Old Testament Library; revd edn; London: SCM Press, 1972).

Reif, S.C., 'A Mission to the Holy Land - 1839', *Transactions of the Glasgow University Oriental Society* 24 (1971-2 [1974]), 1-13.

_____, 'Some Recent Developments in the Study of Medieval Hebrew Liturgy', in N.R.M. de Lange (ed.), *Hebrew Scholarship and the Mediaeval World* (Cambridge: Cambridge University Press, 2001), 60-73.

Renan, Ernest, *Vie de Jésus* (14th edn; Paris: Michel Lévy, 1873).

Richer, Jean, *Sacred Geography of the Ancient Greeks: Astrological Symbolism in Art, Architecture, and Landscape* (tr. Christine Rhone; Albany, NY: State University of New York Press, 1994).

Riesenfeld, H., *The Resurrection in Ezekiel xxxvii and in the Dura-Europos Paintings* (Uppsala Universitets Årsskrift, 11; Uppsala: Almqvist and Wiksell, 1948). (This study is reprinted in J. Gutman [ed.], *No Graven Images: Studies in Art and the Hebrew Bible* [New York: Ktav, 1971].)

Roberts, David, *Yesterday and Today: The Holy Land. Lithographs and Diaries by David Roberts, R.A.* (Text by Fabio Bourbon, Photographs by Antonio Attini. Shrewsbury: Swan Hill Press, 1997).

Robinson, Edward, *Biblical Researches in Palestine, Mount Sinai and Arabia Petraea: A Journal of Travels in the Year 1838*, I (3 vols.; London: John Murray, 1841).

Safrai, S., 'The Holy Congregation of Jerusalem', *ScrHieros* 23 (1972), 62-78.

_____, *Die Wallfahrt im Zeitalter des Zweiten Tempels* (Forschungen zum jüdisch-christlichen Dialog, 3; Neukirchen-Vluyn: Neukirchener Verlag, 1981).

_____, 'Jerusalem in the Halacha of the Second Temple Period', in M. Poorthuis and Ch. Safrai (eds.), *The Centrality of Jerusalem: Historical Perspectives* (Kampen: Kok Pharos, 1996), 94-113.

Safrai, S., and Stern, M. (eds.), *The Jewish People in the First Century: Historical Geography, Political History, Social, Cultural and Religious Life and Institutions*, I (Compendia Rerum Iudaicarum ad Novum Testamentum, I; Assen: Van Gorcum, 1974).

Sanders, E.P., *Paul, the Law, and the Jewish People* (Philadelphia: Fortress/London: SCM, 1983/1985).

_____, 'Jerusalem and its Temple in Early Christian Thought and Practice', in L.I. Levine (ed.), *Jerusalem: Its Sanctity and Centrality to Judaism, Christianity, and Islam* (New York: Continuum, 1999), 90-103.

Sawyer, J.F.A., 'Daughter of Zion and Servant of the Lord in Isaiah: A Comparison', *JSOT* 44 (1989), 89-107.

Schultz, J.P., 'From Sacred Space to Sacred Object to Sacred Person in Jewish Antiquity', *Shofar* 12 (1993), 28-37.

Schwartz, E., and Mommsen, Th. (eds.), *Die Griechischen Christlichen Schriftsteller der Ersten Drei Jahrhunderte. Eusebius*, II.2 (Leipzig: J.C. Hinrichs, 1908).

Scott, J.M., *Geography in Early Judaism and Christianity: The Book of Jubilees* (SNTSMS 113; Cambridge: Cambridge University Press, 2002).

Seybold, K., 'Jerusalem in the View of the Psalms', in M. Poorthuis and Ch. Safrai (eds.), *The Centrality of Jerusalem: Historical Perspectives* (Kampen: Kok Pharos, 1996), 7-14.

Shead, A.G., *The Open Book and the Sealed Book: Jeremiah 32 in its Hebrew and Greek Recensions* (SJSOT 347; London: Sheffield Academic Press, 2002).

Silberman, N.A., *Digging for God and Country: Exploration, Archeology, and the Secret Struggle for the Holy Land 1799-1917* (New York: Doubleday, 1982).

Simpson, W., 'The Middle of the World, in the Holy Sepulchre', *PEFQS* 1888, 260-63.

Sizer, S.R., 'Dispensational Approaches to the Land', in P.S. Johnston and P.W.L. Walker (eds.), *The Land of Promise: Biblical, Theological and Contemporary Perspectives* (Leicester: Apollos, 2000), 142-71.

Smith, W., and Fuller, J.M. (eds.), *A Dictionary of the Bible* (2nd edn; London: John Murray, 1893).

Speiser, E.A., *Genesis* (AB 1; Garden City: Doubleday, 1964).

Stanley, A.P., *Sinai and Palestine in Connection with their History* (23rd edn; London: John Murray, 1918).

Stordalen, T., *Echoes of Eden: Genesis 2-3 and Symbolism of the Eden Garden in Biblical Hebrew Literature* (Contributions to Biblical Exegesis and Theology, 25; Leuven: Peeters, 2000).

Sweeney, M.A., *Berit Olam: Studies in Hebrew Narrative and Poetry: The Twelve Prophets*, II (Collegeville: Liturgical Press, 2000).

Sykes, S., *Time and Space in Haggai-Zechariah 1-8: A Bakhtinian Analysis of a Prophetic Chronicle* (Studies in Biblical Literature, 24; New York: Lang, 2002).

Taylor, Joan E., *Christians and the Holy Places: The Myth of Jewish-Christian Origins* (Oxford: Clarendon, 1993).

Terrien, S., 'The Omphalos Myth and Hebrew Religion', *VT* 20 (1970), 315-38.

Thenius, Otto, 'De Golgotha et Sancto Sepulcro' (short title), *Zeitschrift für die historische Theologie* 12/4 (1842), 3-34.

Thompson, T.L., *The Bible in History: How Writers Create a Past* (London: Jonathan Cape, 1999).

Tilly, M., 'Geographie und Weltordnung im Aristeasbrief', *JSJ* 28 (1997), 131-53.

Tobler, T., and Molinier, A. (eds.), *Itinera Hierosolymitana et Descriptiones Terrae Sanctae* (Publications de la Société de l'Orient Latin, Série Géographique I-II. Itinera Latina, I; Geneva: J.-G. Fick, 1879).

Toorn, K. van der, 'The Babylonian New Year Festival: New Insights from the Cuneiform Texts and their Bearing on Old Testament Study', *SVT* 43 (1991), 331-44.

Tsafrir, Y., 'Jewish Pilgrimage in the Roman and Byzantine Periods', *Akten des XII. Internationalen Kongresses für christliche Archäologie* (Jahrbuch für Antike und Christentum Ergänzungsband, 20, 1; Münster: Aschendorffsche Verlagsbuchhandlung, 1995), 369-76.

Tsumura, D.T., *The Earth and the Waters in Genesis 1 and 2: A Linguistic Investigation* (SJSOT 83; Sheffield: JSOT Press, 1989).

Tucker, G.M., 'Witnesses and "Dates" in Israelite Contracts', *CBQ* 28 (1966), 42-45.

Tuell, S., 'The Rivers of Paradise: Ezekiel 47:1-12 and Genesis 2:10-14', in William P. Brown and S. Dean McBride (eds.), *God Who Creates: Essays in Honor of W. Sibley Towner* (Grand Rapids and Cambridge: Eerdmans, 2000), 171-89.

Vikan, G., 'Pilgrims in Magi's Clothing: The Impact of Mimesis on Early Byzantine Pilgrimage Art', in R. Ousterhout (ed.), *The Blessings of Pilgrimage* (Illinois Byzantine Studies, 1; Urbana and Chicago: University of Illinois Press, 1990), 97-107.

Volz, P., *Der Prophet Jeremia* (KAT 10; Leipzig: A. Deichertsche Verlagsbuchhandlung, 1922).

Vreté, M., 'The Restoration of the Jews in English Protestant Thought 1790-1840', *Middle Eastern Studies* 8 (1972), 3-50.

Wace, H., and Schaff, P. (eds.), *Gregory of Nyssa* (Nicene and Post-Nicene Fathers of the Christian Church [Second Series], 5; Oxford: Parker and Co./New York: Christian Literature Company, 1893).

Walker, P.W.L., *Holy City, Holy Places?: Christian Attitudes to Jerusalem and the Holy Land in the Fourth Century* (Oxford Early Christian Studies; Oxford: Clarendon, 1990).

_____, 'Jerusalem and the Holy Land in the 4th Century', in A. O'Mahony (ed.) with G. Gunner and K. Hintlian, *The Christian Heritage in the Holy Land* (London: Scorpion Cavendish, 1995).

_____, 'The Land in the Apostles' Writings', in P.S. Johnston and P.W.L. Walker (eds.), *The Land of Promise: Biblical, Theological and Contemporary Perspectives* (Leicester: Apollos, 2000), 81-99.

Wallace, H.N., *The Eden Narrative* (Harvard Semitic Monographs, 32; Atlanta: Scholars Press, 1985).

Waltke, B., 'The Phenomenon of Conditionality within Unconditional Covenants', in A. Gileadi (ed.), *Israel's Apostasy and Restoration: Essays in Honor of Roland K. Harrison* (Grand Rapids: Baker Book House, 1988), 123-39.

Watts, J.D.W., *Isaiah 34-66* (WBC 25; Waco: Word Books, 1987).

Weinfeld, M., 'Zion and Jerusalem as Religious and Political Capital: Ideology and Utopia', in R.E. Friedman (ed.), *The Poet and the Historian: Essays in Literary and Historical Biblical Criticism* (Harvard Semitic Studies, 26; Chico: Scholars Press, 1983).

_____, *The Promise of the Land: The Inheritance of the Land of Canaan by the Israelites* (The Taubman Lectures in Jewish Studies, 3; Berkeley: University of California Press, 1993).

_____, 'The Roots of the Messianic Idea', in R.M. Whiting (ed.), *Mythology and Mythologies* (Melammu Symposia, 2; Helsinki: The Neo-Assyrian Text Corpus Project, 2001), 279-87.

Weiser, A., *Die Psalmen. Erster Teil: Psalm 1-60* (4th edn; ATD 14; Göttingen: Vandenhoeck and Ruprecht, 1955).

Wenham, G.J., 'Sanctuary Symbolism in the Garden of Eden Story', *Proceedings of the World Congress of Jewish Studies*, 9 (1986), 19-25.

_____, *Genesis 1-15* (WBC 1; Waco: Word Books, 1987).

White, H.C., *Narration and Discourse in the Book of Genesis* (Cambridge: Cambridge University Press, 1991).

Wilken, R.L., *The Land Called Holy: Palestine in Christian History and Thought* (New Haven: Yale University Press, 1992).

_____, 'Christian Pilgrimage to the Holy Land', in Nitza Rosovsky (ed.), *City of the Great King: Jerusalem from David to the Present* (Cambridge, MA: Harvard University Press, 1996).

Wilkinson, J., 'Christian Pilgrims in Jerusalem during the Byzantine Period', *PEQ* 108 (1976), 75-101.

_____, *Jerusalem Pilgrims Before the Crusades* (Warminster: Aris and Phillips, 1977).

_____, 'Jewish Holy Places and the Origins of Christian Pilgrimage', in R. Ousterhout (ed.), *The Blessings of Pilgrimage* (Illinois Byzantine Studies, 1; Urbana and Chicago: University of Illinois Press, 1990), 41-53.

_____, 'Visits to Jewish Tombs by Early Christians', in *Akten des XII. Internationalen Kongresses für christliche Archäologie*, I (Jahrbuch für Antike und Christentum Ergänzungsband, 20, 1; Münster: Aschendorffsche Verlagsbuchhandlung, 1995), 452-65.

Williamson, P.R., 'Promise and Fulfilment: The Territorial Inheritance', in P.S. Johnston and P.W.L. Walker (eds.), *The Land of Promise: Biblical, Theological and Contemporary Perspectives* (Leicester: Apollos, 2000), 15-34.

Wilson, Sir Charles W., 'Golgotha and the Holy Sepulchre', *PEFQS* 1902, 66-77.

_____, 'Golgotha and the Holy Sepulchre' [*concluded*], *PEFQS* 1904, 26-41.

_____, *Golgotha and the Holy Sepulchre* (ed. C.M. Watson; London: Palestine Exploration Fund, 1906).

Wolff, H.W., *Joel and Amos* (Hermeneia; Philadelphia: Fortress, 1977).

Wright, T., 'Jerusalem in the New Testament', in P.W.L. Walker (ed.), *Jerusalem Past and Present in the Purposes of God* (2nd edn; Carlisle: Paternoster, 1994), 53-77.

Wyatt, N., 'Le centre du monde dans les littératures d'Ougarit et d'Israël', *JNSL* 21 (1995), 123-42.

Zevit, Z., *The Religions of Ancient Israel: A Synthesis of Parallactic Approaches* (London: Continuum, 2001), 405-38.

Zimmerli, W., *Ezechiel, 2: Ezechiel 25-48* (BKAT 13/2; Neukirchen-Vluyn: Neukirchener Verlag, 1969).

Index of Textual References

Biblical

Non-Biblical

Index of Authors

Index of Topics

The Didsbury Lectures published by Paternoster